The EMU Fact Book

NIKI CHESWORTH
AND
SUSIE PINE-COFFIN

**This book was researched and written in the Spring of 1998. As this
was six months before the introduction of EMU some of the content
of this book may be subject to change. The authors have indicated
which aspects of the introduction of the single currency are still
uncertain.**

YOURS TO HAVE AND TO HOLD
BUT NOT TO COPY

First published in 1998

Apart from any fair dealing for the purposes of research or private study, or criticism or review, as permitted under the Copyright, Designs and Patents Act 1988,
this publication may only be reproduced, stored or transmitted, in any form or by
any means, with the prior permission in writing of the publishers, or in the case of
reprographic reproduction, in accordance with the terms and licences issued by
the CLA. Enquiries concerning reproduction outside those terms should be sent
to the publishers at the undermentioned address:

Kogan Page Limited
120 Pentonville Road
London N1 9JN

© Niki Chesworth and Susie Pine-Coffin, 1998

The right of Niki Chesworth and Susie Pine-Coffin to be identified as the authors
of this work has been asserted by them in accordance with the Copyright, Designs
and Patents Act 1988.

British Library Cataloguing in Publication Data

A CIP record for this book is available from the British Library.

ISBN 0 7494 2815 5

Typeset by Saxon Graphics Ltd, Derby
Printed and bound by Clays Ltd, St Ives plc

74658

Contents

Preface – Why You Should Read This Book

You may think that as Britain may not join the single currency for another five years – if at all – you will not be affected by Economic and Monetary Union (EMU). You could not be more wrong. Not only is the introduction of the single currency inevitable, with 11 member states joining from January 1999, but so is the fact that EMU will impact on British businesses and consumers.

Half of Britain's trade is with Europe, including Eire, so anyone importing from or exporting to the Continent will soon come under pressure to price, tender, invoice and accept payments in the new currency – the euro.

Even businesses that trade only in the domestic market will be affected. Several of the largest UK companies will be adopting the euro as their trading currency from January 1999. That means British businesses supplying these large corporations with everything from staff and printing contracts to raw materials and distribution services will come under pressure to do the same. Although there will be no compulsion to adopt the single currency for trading, these large pro-euro companies have warned smaller firms down the supply chain that they will need to trade in euros to remain competitive.

The impact of the single currency does not end there. British business – even those only trading within the UK domestic market – will be affected by:

■ rises and falls in the value of sterling until the UK joins the EMU and British companies can benefit from exchange rate certainty. These currency fluctuations could wipe out profits on exports and price goods out of the domestic market if cheaper imports make your prices uncompetitive

■ increased competition from European companies taking advantage of the benefits of the single currency and the growth in cross-border trade

▌ fluctuations in interest rates

▌ and new European legislation – including an increasing regulatory burden on employers.

That is why it is essential for business to start preparing for the euro as soon as possible. Remember, the future of your business is at stake. Continental firms grabbing the opportunities presented by the single currency could undercut your prices and steal your customers. Single pricing will lead to greater price transparency and unless your prices remain competitive your business will suffer. But aside from ensuring you do not become an EMU loser, you should also take advantage of the benefits of the single currency.

Vernon Ellis, managing director for Europe, the Middle East, Africa and India of Andersen Consulting recently wrote of the single market: 'It is a force which, if harnessed correctly, can become a driver of the virtuous circle of European competitiveness. Equally, a failure to grasp the opportunities presented by EMU will almost certainly mean a failure to build competitiveness.'

Making the most of the euro can bring major benefits to all firms – not just pan-European corporations. You can source your supplies and raw materials in European countries where prices are cheaper, cutting the overheads of running your business. You can take advantage of European grants. And you can exploit the vast new single market to export for the first time, expanding your business into new markets.

Do You Know What You Need to Do to Prepare For the Advent of the European Single Currency Next Year?

According to a number of surveys, the answer for most companies is no. We're heading towards the unknown and that makes people feel uncomfortable.

The pan-European Association of SMEs has, through surveys, identified two key areas that affect businesses preparing for the arrival of the euro.

■ The first is a shortage of practical information about the reality and the impact of EMU on business.

■ The second is fear – no one really knows what the consequences of monetary union will be for Europe over the longer term.

Although this book does not predict a safe landing for EMU, it does aim to overcome these two problems by informing smaller businesses what could affect them in the coming years and what they need to do to be prepared.

How to be a Euro Winner

Only those firms that prepare for the implications of the EMU can reap any benefits. Yet a recent survey found that only one in ten businesses which trade with Europe have made any significant plans for the introduction of the euro. Those with no overseas trade have made even fewer preparations.

In addition, businesses should grab the opportunities the single currency will offer. That could mean moving into new markets, offering new products and services or taking advantage of the massive new Single Market to sell directly to consumers in other countries using eCommerce (sales through the internet) or mail order.

Accountants Grant Thornton – following a recent survey of European companies – has warned that those businesses 'able to adapt quickly and make the necessary changes will have a strong competitive advantage over those that drag their feet'.

As well as answering the questions you should be asking about the introduction of the single currency, this book aims to help businesses to not only survive but thrive after January 1999.

Introduction – A brief guide to EMU

What Does EMU Mean?

Economic and Monetary Union. It is the latest stage in the evolution of European integration. It involves the replacement of local currencies in individual Member States with a single currency – the euro.

From 1 January 1999 the first 11 countries to join EMU will have their local currency exchange rates fixed at set rates to the euro. In 2002 local currencies will then be replaced by the euro. In order to achieve this the economies of Member States will be required to converge, financial prudence will be enforced, government debt reduced and low inflation maintained.

From January 1999 the new European Central Bank (ECB) will set interest rates in these first 11 Member States – not the individual central banks of each country. At the time of writing, interest rates for 'in' countries were to converge at around 3.5 per cent – well below those of Britain.

Who is Joining ERM?

Germany, France, Spain, Italy, Portugal, Belgium, Austria, Luxembourg, Ireland, Finland and The Netherlands. Greece wanted to join but did not qualify. Denmark and Sweden have opted out and the UK has announced its intention to join at a later date.

What is the Euro and How is it Different From the ECU?

The European Currency Unit, the ECU, was introduced alongside the European Monetary System (EMS) to provide a weighted average of EMS currencies. The ECU was not a hard currency with coins or bank notes. However, it is a trading currency. Since 1979 it has been used in commercial financial transactions in the same way as the dollar and the yen are used.

From next year, the ECU will be replaced by the euro. Although one ECU will equal one euro they are calculated differently. The ECU is an average of all EMS currencies. The euro, on the other hand, is the average of only those 11 currencies that join EMU on 1 January 1999.

What is the ERM?

ERM is the exchange rate mechanism created to set the bands for the EMS. It only allows currencies to fluctuate within certain bands. From January 1999 it will be replaced by EMU which introduces fixed exchange rates for the 11 Member States – so currencies will no longer fluctuate within set bands.

In addition there will be ERM2. This will be the exchange rate mechanism for countries not joining EMU in the first wave but wanting to at a later date. ERM2 will replace the current ERM mechanism on 1 January 1999.

Britain is likely to join ERM2 before adopting the single currency. Participation in ERM2 will be voluntary, as with the ERM, and a standard fluctuation band of plus or minus 15 per cent around the central rates will remain (as it is today), although there may be some narrower bands for some currencies.

In principle, if a country is having difficulty keeping within the bands, the ECB will step in to keep them within their trading bands. However both the ECB and non-participating central banks will have the right to suspend intervention unilaterally.

What Other Economic Policy is Part of EMU?

The growth and stability pact calls for greater coordination between Member States to develop economic policies which focus on employment.

It is designed to improve Europe's global competitiveness, giving special attention to labour and product market efficiency, technological innovation and creating more opportunities for small and medium-sized enterprises (SMEs).

What is Britain Going to Do?

In October 1997, Labour outlined its position on joining EMU when the Chancellor of the Exchequer, Gordon Brown, made a statement to Parliament. He said there was no constitutional reason why Britain should not join EMU and that in principle the Labour party was committed to joining, although he ruled out doing so in 1999.

Gordon Brown said the time was not right because having applied the economic tests, 'It is not in this country's interest to join in the first wave of EMU starting on 1 January 1999 and, barring some fundamental and unforeseen change in economic circumstances, making a decision, this Parliament, to join is not realistic.'

In his speech to Parliament, Gordon Brown said:

> In order to give ourselves a genuine choice in the future, it is essential that the Government and business prepare intensively during the Parliament, so that Britain will be in a position to join a single currency, should we wish to, early in the next Parliament.
>
> If a single currency works and is successful, Britain should join it. We should therefore begin now to prepare ourselves so that, should we meet the economic tests, we can make a decision to join a successful single currency early in the next Parliament. At present, with no preparation, it is not a practical option. We must put ourselves in the position for Britain to exercise genuine choice.

The questions of preparation are immense – practical questions for business, as well as for Government. Euro notes and coins will, for example, be circulating across Europe from 1 January 2002. Some companies, like Marks & Spencer, have already decided to prepare to accept euros in Britain. Others will want advice on what is best for them.

Because both the Government and business must prepare intensively during the next few years, Gordon Brown said he will:

▌ commence work on the detailed transition arrangements for the possible introduction of the euro in Britain, including the introduction of notes and coins, should we wish to enter;

▌ help businesses by informing them what they should do now to prepare for the introduction of the euro in 1999, whether we are 'in' or 'out'; and

▌ work with business on what the Government must do to prepare for EMU, should we decide to join it in the next Parliament.

Even if Britain meets its own and the European economic tests for joining EMU, the decision will still be up to the people. A referendum will be held before any decision is made to join.

THE SINGLE CURRENCY TIMETABLE

Chronological Order of Events

1987 The Single European Act establishes the goal of a Single Market in Europe by 1992
1992 The signing of the Treaty on European Union in Maastricht
1993 The EEC becomes the European Union (EU). With it comes the free circulation of goods, services, people and capital
1995 Madrid Summit Meeting (December). The European Council adopts the changeover scenario for the introduction of the euro
1996 Start of the Inter-Governmental Conference (IGC) in Turin (March) – discussion centres around institutional EU reform and enlargement of the EU

1996   Dublin Summit Meeting (December). The European Council determines the legal framework for the introduction of the euro and the continuity of contracts

1997   Confirmation of the Stability and Growth Pact with the Treaty of Amsterdam

1998   The first 11 countries to adopt the single currency were agreed in May. They are: Germany, France, Belgium, Spain, Italy, The Netherlands, Austria, Finland, Portugal, Ireland and Luxembourg. The four Member States of the EU 15 that will not adopt the currency on 1 January 1999 are Britain, Greece, Denmark and Sweden.

1999   1 January:
   ▮ irrevocable fixing of conversion rates for Member States
   ▮ the euro becomes the official currency for all EMU Member States

2002   January (at the latest): euro notes and coins to be introduced

2002   July: all local currencies of EMU members will be withdrawn from circulation

Phase A   May 1998 – 1 January 1999

1.   European Council names the countries which will join EMU on 1 January 1999
2.   Central Bank is established
3.   Businesses accelerate preparation efforts
4.   Financial and banking sectors finalize changeover preparations
5.   Businesses accelerate preparation efforts

Phase B   1 January 1999 – 31 December 2001

1.   Conversion rates of participating countries permanently fixed on 1 January 1999
2.   The euro will be launched as the currency of EMU
3.   National currencies will continue to exist but as expressions of EMU
4.   Monetary, capital, foreign exchange and inter-bank markets will convert to euros. You will have the choice to use either

euros or local currency. A number of multinational companies are expected to switch to trading in euros and are therefore likely to encourage their suppliers and customers to do the same. Most consumers will continue to use their national currency for the time being

Phase C 1 January 2002 – 1 July 2002

1. National currency notes and coins will start to be withdrawn from circulation
2. All participating nations must complete the changeover
3. All assets must be converted into euros
4. In July 2002 all EMU member countries will have their national currencies withdrawn from circulation

1 What EMU Means for Business

The effects on the economies of the 11 Member States joining the single currency on 1 January 1999 – and therefore businesses and consumers throughout the community – should be:

▌ lower inflation – inflation has plagued Europe's economies since the 1970s, which in turn has created even higher levels of unemployment. By setting strict economic criteria on government debt and spending, and by fixing exchange rates, Europe should be in for a period of long-term low inflation

▌ the end of competitive devaluations between European currencies – when a currency is devalued the costs of exports from that country become cheaper. This, in the eyes of some European members, is unfair because it gives the country that has devalued a competitive advantage and inevitably leads to political friction and rivalry. The end of revaluations of currencies will therefore create a more level playing field for trade exchange rate stability – this will reduce the risk of exchange rate fluctuations hitting company profits. However, the UK will not benefit from this until we join EMU.

In the words of Margaret Beckett, former President of the Board of Trade:

The introduction of the single currency will change the business environment not just in those 11 countries, but across the whole of Europe. Europe is going through some exciting changes which could bring real opportunities for businesses who plan and prepare properly, but potential costs and problems for those who put their heads in the sand right across the EU, but nowhere more so than in the UK. All sectors need to think about it carefully, but clearly exporters and importers and those in supply chains will be particularly affected.

How Significant Will the Elimination of Currency Risk be With the Euro-zone?

Historically, severe exchange rate fluctuations have disrupted both trade and investment. Some manufacturers have actually seen profits from exports vanish overnight because the rates have moved. Outside the single currency, exporters have two options to counter the risk of currency volatility. They can either shoulder the risk and take it on the chin, or hedge their financial position and insure against the risk. This second option is complicated and – for most small to medium-sized firms – too expensive to be worth the effort. The problems of dealing with foreign currency have in some cases deterred smaller firms from trading overseas including within the EU.

However for British firms these risks and expenses will not be eradicated until we join the single currency. That means they will be at a competitive disadvantage to Continental competitors who will no longer suffer these costs. For these European companies the trading environment within Europe is likely to change quite radically.

The elimination of currency risk is also expected to sharpen competition by putting downward pressure on prices. More companies are likely to form joint ventures or merge to create economies of scale and thus reduce costs as Europe tries to compete with the emerging markets and their cheap imports.

Apart From the Elimination of Currency Risk, What Other Benefits Will There be for European Businesses?

The principles of the single currency are to create an environment of low inflation, monetary stability and sound public finances.

The hope is that by keeping the lid on inflation and creating a steady, sound economic environment, businesses will prosper, as the European economy as a whole picks up. In turn governments will be encouraged to reform employment law to create a more flexible labour market. Economic pundits are divided on whether this will lead to increased or reduced unemployment. Company mergers and acquisitions and increased competition are expected to lead to higher unemployment. However, on the other hand, economic prosperity should reduce unemployment and – in turn – encourage further economic prosperity.

How will Lower Inflation, Monetary Stability and Sound Public Finances Affect Business?

They should create greater economic stability; this will help both businesses and consumers to plan for the long, rather than short term. By keeping inflation low, interest rates should come down; this will create an environment where businesses and individuals are more likely to invest and save for the future. In turn this should generate economic prosperity, by creating more jobs and a better standard of living for everyone. If consumer demand remains high, businesses will continue to benefit from increasing sales.

Lower interest rates will also mean cheaper loans; this will encourage more people to buy their own homes and businesses to expand.

So How Will This Affect British Businesses – After All We Will Not be Joining EMU Yet?

Although Britain will not be one of the 11 EU Member States adopting the single currency on 1 January 1999, it will nevertheless be affected by this momentous event. Some 50 per cent of British trade is with EU states, many large companies are owned by EU corporations and – with the increasing globalization of world money markets – the strength of Sterling and therefore UK interest rates is dependent on the economic policies adopted by the rest of Europe.

This high level of trade with Europe means many British businesses will be forced to work within a dual currency system. So even if we do not join EMU, a large proportion of our trade will be in euros.

Already Britain is subject to EU laws and further legislation is planned. However, most of this legislation does – and will – affect businesses, for example, the maximum working week.

The euro should help companies to grow, attract investment and reduce trading costs. A European Commission report published in October 1996 claims that since the inception of the Single Market in 1985, approximately 900,000 jobs have been created, GDP has risen from 1.1 to 1.5 per cent and investment levels are 2.7 per cent higher than they would have been without a Single Market.

It also claims that trade within the EU has risen faster than trade between the EU and the rest of the world – with the share of imported manufactured goods coming from the EU rising from 61 per cent in 1985 to 68 per cent in 1995.

In addition direct foreign investment into Europe has jumped from 28 per cent between the years of 1982 and 1987 to 44 per cent during the 1990s. The report also claims that the abolition of trade barriers, such as customs documentation and other formalities within the EU trading bloc, has saved businesses about $3.6 billion a year.

From the corporate sector, British Petroleum's chairman, Sir David Simon, believes that the argument over sovereignty will quickly evaporate when British people have to start paying more for their mortgages or even lose their jobs because, outside EMU, Britain will become less competitive. He believes that joining EMU will provide a great boost to the UK's small and medium-sized businesses. Currently only about 10 per cent of our smaller sized companies trade outside Britain. They are put off by the complexities of dealing with different legal, tax and regulatory systems of foreign partners, and of course the burden of the transaction costs. EMU will put an end to many of these trade barriers.

How Else Could EMU Work for British Businesses?

It has been estimated that our participation in the Single Market provides work for over one million people.

A successful single currency will create more trading opportunities and in turn more jobs, particularly for SMEs whose expansion plans are often hindered by national barriers.

The single currency should reduce the cost of doing business in Europe, reduce inflation and create a sound economic environment by ridding us of the boom-bust cycle which to date has crippled so many companies.

For the last 20 years, British interest rates have averaged 3.5 per cent more than those in Germany; this has put Sterling at an immediate competitive disadvantage with Germany.

The single currency will also aid euro-trade giving British companies greater access to the 370 million consumers living in the EU. As almost 60 per cent of Britain's trade and capital flows is dependent on these countries any reduction in the costs of trade will help companies to compete.

If Britain Isn't Going to Join EMU in the Immediate Future, Why is the Euro Going to be an Issue?

While the UK stays out of EMU, we won't be forced to use euros although the euro will become an important trading currency from January 1999.

For a start, many businesses trading with companies within the euro bloc or with European multinational companies in the UK, may find it easier to use euros rather than Sterling. Businesses in the tourism sector or with retail outlets in areas that are visited by a number of European tourists may also find it beneficial to be able to deal in euros.

There are two reasons for this. First, if you deal with companies either in Europe or in the UK that adopt the euro as their trading currency you could come under pressure to price and trade in euros. Secondly, even if you do not come under pressure to adopt the euro you may find that by doing so you can boost European trade.

So Could Businesses Suffer if They Don't Adopt the Euro?

Yes – some could. Several major corporations are planning to adopt the euro from January 1999 as a trading currency. If you cannot price in euros and do not have the accountancy and banking facilities to cope with the new currency you could suffer if your trading partners would prefer to deal only in euros.

Even if you do not come under pressure to use euros, companies you supply may decide to tender for contracts or compare different prices of goods and services in euros. This is because the single currency will make price comparisons much easier – known as transparent pricing. If you cannot quote in euros you could miss out. Or you could lose existing business because you have not done your homework to find out whether or not your euro prices are competitive.

Will Businesses Suffer Because Britain Does Not Join EMU?

Sadly, the answer to this could be yes – unless the EMU turns out to be a disaster. Our European competitors will benefit from low currency exchange costs and will no longer suffer from exchange rate fluctuations when trading with other 'in' states. British companies will still have to suffer these costs. And if Sterling remains strong there will be the added disadvantage that British goods are more expensive abroad.

The single currency has also led to lower inflation and lower interest rates in other EU states. While UK inflation is still low, our interest rates are much higher than on the Continent. Until Britain moves towards membership of EMU (when our interest rates are likely to fall), businesses will suffer higher borrowing costs.

Only if the single currency is a disaster will British businesses be better off. But even then, what affects Europe is likely to affect the UK so there will still be some impact on British firms. However, this scenario is unlikely in the short term because there is too much political will behind making the single currency work.

So British Businesses Will Pay More Because Britain is Staying Out of EMU?

Continental firms adopting the euro will have much lower exchange costs than British businesses. But this is not the only cost. British firms will also have to suffer from any fluctuations in the value of the euro against the pound. They could also be put at a disadvantage to European competitors because Continental firms will have cheaper and more readily available capital at their disposal, due to lower interest rates and deeper, more liquid capital markets.

However, if we stay out of EMU for good, we'll be able to avoid the most expensive exercise and that's the introduction of the new currency, unless of course you are a retailer or business that decides to run a dual pricing structure anyway.

But my Business Does Not Trade Overseas, So How Can I be Affected?

If Sterling remains high and so do British interest rates, goods from overseas become cheaper. So you could find that you are priced out of your own domestic market. Remember, just because you have not planned to take advantage of the single currency does not mean companies you supply are also burying their heads in the sand.

The chances are that all major British companies will be looking to derive as much benefit as possible from the single currency. As such they will probably start to look for cheaper suppliers in EU states as barriers to trade are removed.

Margaret Beckett, former President of the Board of Trade warned:

> Many businesses trading solely in the UK may feel that as they do not currently export they are immune. But the transparency of prices that the euro will bring will affect them too. Competitors from elsewhere in the EU may well emerge. Or they may discover that they have opportunities to get into new markets themselves. What effects will the euro have on

their rivals' competitive strategy and how if need be should they counter this?

Transparent pricing offers some threats, which firms need to be ready for, but also – for competitive UK firms – it offers huge opportunities. Every management and every board in every firm in the country should be thinking through what the euro will mean for them both practically and strategically.

So Even Though Britain Isn't Going to Join EMU in the Foreseeable Future, I Need to Start Preparing Now?

Yes. As explained above, we are vulnerable to the impact of EMU. While it is tempting to ignore it in the hope that it'll go away, it won't.

✦ So What Should a British-based Business Do?

As you read on, this book will give you further details on what to do, but first and foremost, accept that EMU is going to be a reality.

The first thing to do is to actively look for information about the euro and EMU and what is being done to deal with the changeover process. For example banks, management consultants, professional advisory bodies, trade associations, accountants, lawyers and official bodies such as the Inland Revenue and Department of Trade and Industry are mostly taking the issue very seriously. Most of the larger organizations should have information that will help you to make the transition.

The next step is for you to think about your long-term business objectives and how they might be affected by the introduction of the euro. If you plan now, you should be able to reap the benefits of a single currency and minimize your adaptation costs.

How Do I Approach the Changeover to EMU?

This very much depends on your individual business, and by reading on we hope to address most of the key issues that could affect your business. However, it is important to note that whether Britain joins EMU or not, it will have a significant impact on our economy and will therefore affect us all in one way or another.

Have Some Companies Already Started Preparing for EMU?

Yes, a number of companies and financial institutions have already started preparing for it. For instance, most banks, both here and in Continental Europe, are providing new products and services to be able to deal with euros from 1 January 1999.

There is a phrase, 'no compulsion, no prohibition', that is commonly used when talking about EMU. Most banks will fully implement this principle for the use of the euro and they'll be in a position to offer their customers payment instruments that will allow them to complete transactions in euros from next year (see Chapter 5, Banking).

A number of multinational companies with subsidiaries in the UK have also indicated that they'll switch to using euros; that means they'll file their accounts, tax declarations and conduct much of their business in euros. That's likely to have a profound effect on other companies in the UK doing business with them and may even lead to a number of them also switching to euros. This will have a domino effect and could lead to even the smallest businesses switching to euros.

Businesses involved in the tourist trade may also change over to the euro quite quickly because of the benefits involved in reducing exchange transaction fees. It'll also reduce their exposure to foreign exchange instability.

What Does 'No Compulsion, No Prohibition' Mean?

It means that anyone who wishes to do so, provided all parties involved in a transaction agree, can opt to use the euro for paper payments rather than their national currency from January 1999. After 2002 the euro bank notes and coins will be introduced to replace the national currencies of the EMU member countries so the phrase becomes irrelevant after this time.

What Impact Will EMU Have on my Business Borrowing Costs?

History shows that borrowing patterns are closely linked to inflation. While Britain struggles to keep the lid on inflation it will be difficult for lenders to offer long-term fixed rate loans instead of variable loans that are subject to short-term interest rate movements.

EMU is offering the potential for creating an environment for long-term periods of low inflation. This will cushion lenders and enable them to offer borrowers long-term fixed rate loans with longer maturity structures. However, while the UK is outside EMU we may not see these benefits – low inflation and low interest rates – for some time. This will put British businesses at a competitive disadvantage to European companies that can borrow and raise finance more cheaply.

What Impact Will There be on Exchange Costs?

As stated above, while the UK is outside EMU we will not benefit from no exchange rate risks or exchange costs. However, if you travel regularly across Europe on business – or transfer money from one 'in' state to another – you will benefit from these savings.

It's been estimated that someone who travelled through all 11 EMU member countries changing money as they went in 1998 would lose 40 per cent of the value of their money at bureaux de change en route.

Once – and if – the UK joins EMU the currency exchange savings for a small business trading with Europe will make a significant difference to bottom line profits. It's been reported that the cost of exporting for a small company is ten times that of a large multinational which can off-set sales against purchases in the same currency and command the best exchange rates.

What Business Opportunities Will EMU Present?

The EMU should also open up new business opportunities for businesses looking to expand because:

▌ it'll eventually be easier for small firms to raise funds – (see Chapter 5, Banking)

▌ Europe will become a single trading bloc with greater transparency. So if your product is in demand and the price is right you'll be able to compete on a level playing field in a much larger market

▌ all business across Europe will be subject to the same employment regulation contained in the Social Chapter – again helping to level the playing field.

All the above will be good news if you're responsive to the new opportunities presented by EMU, efficient and customer-oriented. However, if you're not, your company will come under increasing competition and could find itself out of business.

What Threats to My Business do I Need to Know About?

Once – and if – we join EMU the cost of conversion is going to be high. The British Retailing Consortium alone estimates it will cost British retailers up to £3.5 billion if you include the cost of educating customers, changing labels, training staff, changing computer software and adjusting tills.

Proponents of EMU claim that the costs will be outweighed by the increase in economic growth brought about by lower interest rates and transaction saving costs.

The other threat is to the inward investment we have successfully attracted from the rest of the world. This helps all firms down the supply chain including smaller businesses who supply these major employers. Will companies still see any advantages in setting up factories here? Or will they opt for countries within euro-land so that they can reap the benefits of the European market? Fortunately, the decision on where to base a major company will not just depend on whether or not a particular country is a member of EMU. Our low corporate tax rates and skilled workforce are in our favour. High wage costs and skill shortages in some sectors will work against us.

Although many small firms do not feel that issues such as this are relevant to them, you should look at the risks your business could face should one or more of your major customers decide to relocate their factories/offices/headquarters in another European country.

However, the more immediate threat is that European competitors will 'steal' your customers by offering no exchange-risk euro prices, which are cheaper than yours thanks to the strength of Sterling, which is pricing British goods out of overseas markets. This threat applies even if you trade only within the domestic market. Companies you supply with goods and services will not only be able to source these from cheaper Continental markets but will find trading easier and cheaper.

So is the Euro Likely to be a Strong or a Weak Currency and How Will This Affect Sterling?

There are widely differing views on this. Some economists think that the European Central Bank will opt for making the euro a strong currency to guard against the risk of inflation and to build up its credibility in the market; others think that politicians will want a weak currency against the dollar to help boost European exports.

So the answer is, no one really knows. But if you follow classic economic theory, tight fiscal policy should weaken the value of the euro. However, as the euro is likely to become a strong competitor for the dollar as an international trading currency, demand for the euro is likely to be high and this will push up its value. The determining factor will be the institutional investors and the world's central banks. If they decide the euro is looking attractive and use it as a reserve currency, it'll end up being a strong currency. If this is the case, British exporters will not suffer as a result of high Sterling in comparison to the euro. However, those firms buying raw materials or procuring other goods and services from Europe will find that these are more expensive.

Is the Euro Likely to be a Volatile Currency?

If we look at the performance of the deutschmark against the yen and the dollar over the last three decades and assume the euro will reflect the deutschmark's performance, the answer is yes. However, British businesses are mainly worried about the performance of Sterling versus the euro. Remember, even if you trade only within the domestic market and are pressured to price in euros your profits will be affected by any volatility. See Chapter 3 on adopting the euro and Chapter 8 for details of how to protect your business against exchange rate risks.

Surely British Businesses Will be Better off Being Out of EMU as We Won't be Burdened with New European Bureaucracy?

Euro-sceptics argue that British businesses will have a competitive edge because we'll avoid being burdened with Europe's unemployment problems, bureaucratic and rigid policies.

However, this is rather simplistic. Britain is already adopting, or planning to adopt, much of the European legislation on employment rights – reducing the working week, introducing the minimum wage, increasing maternity benefits and allowing workers to bring unfair dismissal claims after only one year in employment instead of two. So in effect, British businesses will be saddled with much of the European Social Chapter requirements whether or not we join EMU.

2 Business Preparations for EMU

As discussed in the last chapter, for many businesses the issue of whether or not Britain joins EMU is largely academic. The fact that we are part of the EU and 11 of our major trading partners will be adopting the euro from 1 January 1999, means British businesses – even those trading only in the domestic market – could be affected from that date onwards. The only way to assess how your business could lose or gain is by being aware of the threats and opportunities EMU presents.

I'm a Euro-sceptic and Don't Want to Waste Time on Preparing for the Euro; Why Should I Start Thinking About it Now?

If you're trading with Europe or UK-based businesses that are switching to the euro, you've passed the point of no return. Fighting and ignoring EMU now is a waste of time unless you want to try and stop Britain joining EMU. Even if you take this line, you may still have to prepare your business for the inevitable changes to the European trading environment, so ignore it at your peril.

Why Should I Consider Allocating Resources to EMU Now When Britain isn't Going to Join for the Next Few Years at Least?

A stitch in time saves nine. If you leave it until the last minute you'll be more likely to make mistakes. Everyone else will be scrambling to get their businesses ready, and outside consultants will have their hands full working for existing clients so you'll be unlikely to find the best help in the market. It's also likely to cost you more.

If you start preparing for it now, your staff will be ready, your business will be ready and if you need to change over your computer and accounting systems you can look at the issues that'll need to be addressed to deal with the Millennium bug problem at the same time. In the long run this will save you money and should give you a competitive edge when the crunch comes.

Surveys indicate that the British public and some businesses have an alarmingly low level of awareness when asked about EMU and what they think about it. As an employer you have a vested interest in raising awareness amongst your workforce about how it will impact on both your business and your staff.

Where Should I Start?

A lot depends on how big your business is and what expertise you have at your disposal, but remember your staff are the life blood of your business so get them involved in preparing your company for EMU.

If you have not already done so, think about setting up your own EMU project or checklist to assess if and how the euro could affect your business. You should involve those involved in different aspects of your business – IT, accountancy, marketing and sales, distribution and personnel – as the EMU could affect all of these areas.

A good starting place would be for you to arrange a meeting with your partners, other directors, key personnel and/or your business advisers. Some of the main areas you should consider in this meeting are as follows.

▮ Will your business partners, customers, suppliers, etc. start using euros – if so will it mean that if you want to stay competitively viable you have to switch to a dual pricing system?

▮ Will the euro create new export opportunities?

- Is it likely to create more competition in your market?

- How is it likely to affect your existing products and services?

- Will it open up new opportunities for product development?

- Will you have to adjust some of your existing products and services?

- Will it affect your procurement policy?

- What information will you need to provide for your staff, customers, suppliers, etc?

- What impact will it have on your accounting and taxation processes?

- How will it affect your existing business contracts and new business contracts? Are there any other legal considerations that may affect you, such as employment law; will you need to re-denominate your share capital, etc?

- How will it affect your information systems?

- What structures do you need to set up in order to implement and manage the changeover process to the single currency? Should you – or another key member of staff – take on the responsibility for overseeing any changes that need to be made to cope with the euro?

External issues you should be considering are listed below.

Banking

- Will you need a bank account to receive and make payments in euros?

- What will it cost for your bank to provide you with this service and are there any opportunities to cut the costs of paying/accepting payments in euros?

- Can your bank offer you any support and guidance in switching to the use of euros?

Legal/Accounting

▪ Will you need to review existing contracts?

▪ Will the euro affect your existing accounting systems?

▪ What is the optimal date to convert to using euros?

▪ Are there any legal implications if you switch to using euros?

▪ When and how can you use the euro in accounts and tax returns?

▪ What are the requirements for account certification during the transition period?

Pricing

▪ When are your major customers/suppliers likely to switch to using euros?

▪ When should you start invoicing in euros/dual pricing? What factors are likely to influence this decision?

▪ What costs will be involved in dual pricing/switching to euros?

Taxation

▪ Will the euro increase the risk of error – what safeguards can you introduce to minimize the risk?

▪ Can you write off some of the costs of conversion against your profit and loss account?

▪ Will you have assets or liabilities in currencies of the new EMU member countries?

▪ Would making tax declarations in euros be easier than in national currencies?

▪ Will you be taxed if conversion and rounding of currencies into euros creates a capital gain?

IT systems

▪ Will your accounting software be able to cope with the euro?

■ Will your IT provider be able to provide new euro-compatible software? And at what cost?

■ Are your administration systems capable of working in a dual currency environment?

■ Can you use the euro as an opportunity to upgrade your current software and maintenance contracts?

■ Can you link euro conversion needs with your Millennium requirements?

Training

■ Will you need to provide staff with training so they know about the euro, when they should quote euro prices and what your company's policies will be on the euro?

■ Who should you be training – and when?

■ Will you need to arrange training for your customers/suppliers?

■ How much will this cost?

Communications

■ With whom do you need to communicate – suppliers, customers, accountants, marketing/PR/advertising consultants, sales staff, etc?

■ What are the key messages you need to convey?

■ How are you going to advise your customers and suppliers that you are switching to using the euro?

■ What tools, methods will you use to communicate – newsletter, press release, seminar, etc?

■ How much will this cost?

Marketing and sales

■ Will you need to change existing documentation to incorporate the euro?

▎ Can you use the euro as a marketing tool?

▎ Do you need to provide customers with help and information about the euro?

Procurement

▎ Can you find new suppliers at more competitive prices?

▎ Does the euro offer you an opportunity to renegotiate your existing contracts and review price agreements?

▎ If you switch to new suppliers will this affect storage, distribution and/or despatching warehouses?

The more people you consult, the less likely you are to overlook anything.

3 *If, When and How – Using the Euro*

This chapter looks at whether you need to start using the euro for some business transactions, when you may need to start doing so and how to go about adopting the euro and its implications on your business.

Will Other Companies Ask Me to Start Pricing, Paying or Accepting Payments in Euros From Next January?

This will depend on the companies you deal with. If you trade with other European companies they may prefer you to price in euros from next January. Smaller businesses on the Continent are unlikely to make the switch until nearer 2002.

Some large UK corporations are planning to adopt the euro as a trading currency from next January. In turn companies that supply these corporations may come under pressure to do the same. This will have a knock-on effect right down the supply chain. So even if you only trade with a UK company that in turn trades with a UK corporation trading in euros you may find that you have to prepare your business for the euro.

The only way you will find out will be by asking questions now. The sooner you find out what impact the euro will have on your business, the longer you have to prepare and spot any business opportunities.

Will I be Forced to Adopt the Euro?

No – not for the moment. If you trade with European companies you have until 2002 when local currencies will no longer exist. If you only trade in the domestic market you have until after the UK joins EMU and then replaces Sterling with the euro.

However, while there is no compulsion to adopt the euro you may find that by doing so you keep your customers happy, reduce trading costs and win a competitive advantage.

So it is Unlikely the Companies I Deal With Will Switch All Trades to Euros Immediately – Will I Still Have a Choice?

Companies in EMU states have three years to make the transition, and euro notes and coins won't be in circulation until 2002, so no one will actually have euros in their pockets for another three years. Also, the public bodies of some member countries won't be ready to accept payment of taxes or accounts in euros from 1999, so the physical changeover on this side is likely to be slower.

UK companies adopting the euro as a trading currency will also have at least some payments in Sterling – whether they like it or not. Staff will still be paid in Sterling, anything bought by consumers will still be in local currency and any cash expenditure will have to be in pounds and pennies as there will be no actual euro currency until 2002. However, these companies may prefer that larger contracts are denominated in euros. But the 'no compulsion no prohibition' rule will mean you cannot be forced to tender, price or invoice in euros.

What Will Happen in January 2002; Will I be Forced to Switch to Euros?

After 1 January 2002, if you're trading with an EMU member country you will be obliged to use euros rather than their former national currency. So no more dealings in the deutschmark, franc, lire, guilder, etc. It'll be just one basket currency for all. This is good because it should help you to reduce your currency risk exposure, but effectively it won't make much difference; the real difference will come on 1 January 1999 when all the euro-land currencies become fixed against the euro.

From this moment on, you'll find it much easier to compare prices within euro-land because EMU member country currencies will be running in parallel with the euro so you can easily compare the cost of widgets from France with those supplied from Germany.

The difficulty will be when you have to do the same in reverse. Pricing your products to sell into Europe means you'll have to convert your prices to euros too and as the pound is going to be fluctuating up and down against the euro, that could be tricky. Read Chapter 4, Pricing, for further information on this subject.

Why was the Three-year Transitional Period Introduced?

Only the ECB has the power to authorize the issue of euro banknotes and Member States can only issue euro coins with the approval of the ECB. The ECB only existed six months before the introduction of the single currency because it could not be put together until the member countries were confirmed – it is represented by the central banks of the 11 member countries. It would not be physically possible to produce and distribute the volume of banknotes and coins that will be needed in just six months. In 1996 there were about 12.5 billion banknotes circulating within the European Union with a further 8.5 billion notes in store – that takes quite a lot of printing.

Although the process of designing, producing and distributing the euro started in 1996, it was anticipated it would take about five years to complete. The political ramifications of delaying EMU until 2001/2002 were unacceptable to Europe's politicians so the solution decided upon was to allow the single currency to exist as a means of payment without any cash legal tender. That's why we have the situation whereby the euro will exist for non-cash payments from January 1999, running in parallel as the legal equivalent to currencies of EMU members.

Will Coping with Two Currency Units on a Parallel Basis Become Very Complicated?

For a company that is only used to dealing with one currency it will be, but for those who already trade in and use several different currencies it'll be much easier.

I've Heard the Term 'Fungibility of Payments'; What Does That Mean?

'Fungibility of payments' basically means a contract of payments. So until the year 2002, you can choose whether or not you want to pay in euros or the currency of the country in which you owe money.

This means that when you're paying by inter-bank transfers where no money is physically exchanged (cashless transactions) a mechanism has been set up to ensure that each EMU member country has a national currency unit that can be treated as being fungible (replaced) with the euro. This can also be applied to the payee, but only if as a British company you are amenable to it. If not, the counter-party, subject to contract, will have to pay you in Sterling if that is what was initially agreed.

This clause 'Fungibility of payments' also means that the bank of the creditor will have to convert the sum received into the denomination of the creditor's account. So the amount received will be in the original currencies named in the contract. Alternatively the bank will have to re-denominate the transaction into euros if that is what both parties would like. While the banks will be obliged to handle the currency switches that may be requested, they don't have to do it for nothing and there will be an element of 'rounding' on the conversion.

Fungibility of payments is not applicable when payment is made by cheque.

Ultimately if you, as a British citizen or company, owe money to a company or person in an EMU member country you'll be subject to the laws of the country in which your debt is based. This is known as the 'law of money', or 'lex monetae'; this also means the currency denomination of the debt too.

What Does 'Rounding' Mean?

This is the term that's given to the conversion of currencies when the decimal places are rounded up – or down.

When converting to and from euros six significant digits will be used. The result will then be rounded to the nearest euro cent or penny.

Who Will Bear the Cost of Rounding?

The holder of the account whether it's a bank, business or private individual. However, the costs are expected to be small; estimates are that the loss on 2 million euros would be less than 1 euro.

Are There Any Laws on Rounding?

There is an article within the regulations on EMU known as Article 235 Regulation. This Article contains detailed provisions, which set out how the conversions of a currency will be effected, and the circumstances that will allow for a conversion to be rounded off to the nearest cent.

These rules on conversion are not compulsory, at least they're technically not compulsory from the standpoint of criminal law, but if you want to ensure that the converted amount is the legal equivalent of another denomination within the single currency, then you have to adhere to the rules laid out in Article 235.

For example, if you're paying a debt in euros and the currency conversion has not been done within Article 235's guidelines which are part of the provisions laid down in Article 109/(4) Regulation, you run the risk of being seen not to have discharged your debt. So the implications are serious and could be expensive.

Likewise, a bank receiving payment on your or the creditor's behalf won't have fulfilled its obligations to the creditor if it has not followed the prescribed rules when converting the payment back to the currency unit in which the creditor's account is denominated.

What are the Rules of Conversion?

Conversion rates have to be expressed in terms of 1 euro and that's adopted within six significant figures, no more no less, rather than to the decimal point. The currency unit of 1 euro is subdivided into 100 cents.

Conversion is going to be a very complex procedure and will require systems that can adapt to the new conversion rules, particularly if you need to reconcile your accounts on an automated basis. If this is the case and you don't have the in-house resources to deal with it, you should seek advice from your legal adviser or accountant on the best way to deal with this issue. Software suppliers are also updating their programs to cope, so you may find you can buy an off-the-shelf package. See Chapter 7, Information Technology Issues.

In summary, the Regulation requires rounding to be applied where amounts are 'to be paid or accounted for'. This means that when you pay or receive a converted amount it will be necessary to round it to the nearest sub-unit of the currency into which the conversion is to be made, because it won't be possible to convert it to pay a fraction of say a pfennig, a centime or a euro cent. In such cases, the amounts will be rounded up or down.

Will I Have to Pay Commission to Convert Currencies Into Euros?

There are no rules on this, not yet at least. The general view is that market forces will dictate the outcome to this question.

Some banks in EMU Member States are likely to offer euro conversion from the local currency at low cost or free of charge, but they may charge for euro conversions for other currencies. The competition between the banks is going to be fierce, so unless they club together and create an unwritten cartel, market forces should keep the costs down.

As the UK is not a member of EMU, British banks are likely to treat the euro as any other foreign currency and charge the same costs.

What Happens if I am Obliged to Have an ECU (European Currency Unit) Contract Before the Euro is Introduced?

The ECU is not a physical currency as such; it's an expression for a basket of currencies made up of the 15 EU Member States. It was originally designed to be an official accounting unit for EU budgetary purposes and has since been adopted as a unit of account for the private sector.

The ECU will become a currency in its own right, in the form of the euro on 1 January 1999, with 1 ECU equivalent to 1 euro. So if your contract is priced in ECUs it should simply be converted to euros from 1 January 1999 with no difference in the value.

Is it Likely That the British Government Will Introduce New Laws as a Result of EMU?

Yes, it may have to. For example, it may change the law to enable directors of a publicly quoted company to re-denominate their existing share capital.

How Will the Euro Affect my Cash Flow and Working Capital?

If you're trading with overseas partners, you probably monitor the balance in each of your currency accounts to avoid excess cash in one account and an overdraft in the other. If you have bank accounts in more than one other European currency you can combine these into one euro account, getting round this problem and cutting exchange fees on currency transactions.

This in turn will help other aspects of financial planning. If you hedge your currency risks or take out futures and options to hedge the risk of commodity or raw material prices, these can be simplified by having to hedge in just euros.

So I Can Use the Euro to Reduce my Hedging Costs?

If you do any business within the new euro-zone the single currency will fundamentally affect the range of hedging agreements that you've historically had to have in relation to your borrowings, trading and other financial arrangements. As all the euro-zone currencies will effectively become one, this should significantly reduce your hedging costs.

Hedging against currency fluctuation risk typically costs smaller businesses between 1 and 2 per cent of the transaction, so the savings created by EMU could be substantial.

Within the Euro-zone Interest Rates are Likely to be Lower than in Britain; How Can I Benefit From This?

In the longer run, Britain will have to reduce its interest rates to those set by the European Central Bank which currently has a rate of just 3.5 per cent. So long-term fixed-rate borrowing at the UK's current high rates may not be in your best interests. In the short term, however, you may want to protect yourself against any more hikes in the UK base rate.

The other option is to consider borrowing from a European bank which has cheaper rates. This will only be possible if you have a business based in another European country. If you have substantial trade with a particular country you could consider setting up a subsidiary there to get access to cheaper borrowing rates. However, for small firms the costs of this and the additional regulatory burden may outweigh any savings in borrowing costs – assuming a foreign bank will lend to your business.

What Sort of Questions Should I be Asking to Prepare my Financial Operations for EMU?

▌ Will I need to change the services that my bank provides, eg pooling, netting, automatic exchange of balances?

▌ Can I modify the existing procedures I use for paying an invoice/issuing an invoice in a foreign currency? Receiving payments?

▌ Which hedging facilities can I ditch?

▌ During the transition period should I treat the euro as an additional currency or a reference currency for netting/pooling?

▌ Can I reduce the number of bank accounts I currently use?

▌ Can I cut the number of banks I use?

▌ How will the euro change my existing banking relationships; can I use it to reduce my banking fees?

▌ Will my bank try and charge me extra for the euro conversion process?

▌ Will I have to arrange training for my staff so that they're better equipped to deal with the new trading environment?

4 *Pricing*

The euro will impact on prices in two ways – one practical and one fundamental to the survival of your business.

▌ Businesses will have to price goods and services in euros once the UK joins the EMU and some will come under pressure to euro-price from 1999. This is mainly an information technology, accounting and banking problem with firms also having to consider how they display prices in brochures and marketing literature and on shop shelves.

▌ Businesses are likely to come under pressure to reduce prices. The introduction of the euro will lead to price transparency across the 'in' Member States. This combined with increased competition as trade increases will mean *all* UK businesses – even those that only operate in the domestic market – will have to re-assess their pricing policies from 1999 if not before.

When Will I Have to Start Pricing my Goods/Services in Euros?

You may not be able to wait until the euro is adopted in the UK. Pricing in euros may be forced upon you well before then. 'For commercial reasons, companies may use the euro even if their home country is not part of EMU, for instance if all your main competitors do so, or your market is moving towards the euro', says the FEE Euro Information Service.

So I May Have to Adopt the Euro Before the UK Joins the EMU?

Yes. If all your competitors are pricing in euros, you may come under pressure to do the same. Likewise, if a company you supply has adopted the euro you may be asked to tender or price your goods in euros – even if you are supplying another UK company and even if the UK has not yet joined the EMU.

I Thought Only Businesses that Traded With Other European Countries Were Affected

They will be affected first – probably from 1 January 1999. If they are supplying a European company, that company may ask for goods/services to be priced in euros to help them compare prices from different European suppliers. Although this may not happen immediately, it will happen. So it is better to start preparing now.

Senior industrialists have warned that the euro will enter the UK economy 'by the back door' – even if we do not join the single currency. Directors of ICI and Siemens, the German engineering company, recently told the Commons Treasury committee that they expected increasing numbers of their UK suppliers to start pricing in euros from next year. This is expected to have a ripple effect throughout the economy. Richard Sykes, ICI's vice-president responsible for information technology, told the committee that significant parts of the British economy outside the City would become 'euro-liquid'.

Although neither ICI nor Siemens will force UK suppliers to operate in euros they will be looking to purchase in euros whenever possible as a natural hedge against currency risks. This means that companies operating in the domestic market will inevitably be forced to join those firms trading in Europe and adopt the euro. Dixons expects to have to invest at least £20 million to prepare for the introduction of EMU even though it is a domestic-based business and is unlikely to see any benefit.

So Does That Mean EMU Will Cost me Money Even if Britain Does Not Adopt the Euro and I Don't Trade in Europe?

Yes. If like Dixons you expect to have to adapt your accounting systems to cope with euro pricing.

Are There Any Other Pitfalls I Need to Know About?

In addition to being forced to price in euros – even if you only trade within Britain – you could lose business.

M&S has warned that if the pound continues at its current level it may have to review its sourcing policy. That means that instead of sourcing most of its products from the UK it could look to Europe. Robert Colvill, finance director of M&S, told the Commons Treasury committee in March 1998 that the retailer's main worries were uncertainty over the timing of UK entry and the possibility that Sterling would join at too high a rate. He warned: 'We would have to accelerate plans, but not change our plans, for where we would source supplies.'

Other companies are likely to adopt a similar approach to M&S. So if you want your business to remain competitive, price cuts may be forced upon you – even if Britain does not join the EMU.

Surely I Won't be Forced to Adopt the Euro?

No, you won't be forced to do so. You may just come under commercial pressure to adopt the euro.

Companies adopting the euro, including Siemens UK that dealt with 12,000 UK suppliers in 1997 spending some £1.2 billion, insist there will be no compulsion. Bernd Euler, finance director, says: 'We will not use any pressure on our customers or suppliers to deal with us in euros. We will have significant business over the next years in Sterling. We have to pay our employees in pounds, so we need turnover in pounds.'

However, companies may gain a competitive advantage by adopting the euro. So it may be a commercial decision rather than one that is forced upon businesses.

I Only Deal with Consumers not Companies, so Will I Come Under Immediate Pressure to Price in Euros?

No. If you deal mainly with European end-users you will probably not have to price in euros.

Even in Member States that join on the first wave in January 1999, there will be no hard currency until 2002. Until then euros will only be adopted for electronic payments. However, some customers may ask for a euro price – but will not want to actually pay in euros – as they will want to compare prices across Member States to get the best deal.

My Customers Can Already Cross-border Shop for Cheaper Goods if They Want, so Why Should the Introduction of the Euro Make any Difference?

Transparent pricing will not mean shoppers will drive hundreds of miles to buy their groceries more cheaply. But when they are buying larger more expensive items and goods that are easy to ship and transport or can give greater savings, they may consider cross-border shopping. For example, car buyers may find they can buy a vehicle for 40 per cent less in another European state. This is already the case but few manage to take advantage of the savings.

However, increased publicity following the introduction of the euro could encourage more consumers to shop around. Transparent pricing will make it far easier to compare prices and therefore far easier to see what the savings are. Even without the euro, there is already increased cross-border trade in cases where the savings make it worthwhile. Just look at the vast amount of alcohol and tobacco transported from the Continent!

So if I Keep my Prices Competitive, Quote in Euros and Undercut European Rivals, Surely I Can't Lose?

Nice thought, but sadly it's not the case. Although Europe will become one large market we are still in a global economy. Imports in the EU from Southeast Asia have doubled in the last few years and cheap imports from former Eastern Bloc countries are increasing rapidly. This means you must not only look at the prices of European competitors but also global competitors.

Will I Have to Single-price my Goods Across Europe?

No. There are no rules requiring you to have one price. However, while you will not be required to by law, commercial pressures are likely to dictate that there is greater harmonization of prices across Europe.

But I May Have to Reduce Price Differentials in Different European Countries?

While transparent pricing will (when it is adopted across Europe) make it easier for you to compare prices and get the best deal for your business, it will also make it easier for your customers to do the same.

So you could come under pressure to reduce your prices if your business customers complain that they are being charged more than the other companies you supply in other European countries. If you consider this to be unlikely, just think what you would do in the same situation. Any opportunity to put pressure on your suppliers to reduce their prices is worth a try.

I Still Think the Euro Will Not Affect my Prices. I Already Have to be Competitive and if my Business Customers Could Get a Cheaper Rate in Another European State They Would Have Done so Already

True. As recent trade figures show, the strong value of the pound is already hitting British exports. So yes, European companies are already shopping around.

However, transparent pricing will make this easier. And remember it is not just the euro itself that will have an impact. Its introduction is designed to make inter-European trade easier and as such should encourage more trade and therefore more competition. Companies in states that join on the first wave of the single currency will see substantial savings in exchange costs and will no longer suffer losses caused by currency fluctuations. If they pass these savings on to the customer they could under-cut your prices.

But my Contracts State That the Price is Fixed – So How Can I be Pressured to Reduce the Price of my Goods?

Contracts should not be affected by the single currency. European legal advice is that if your contract is for a set price in say deutschmarks, it will simply revert to the same value in euros. So companies you supply cannot claim that the contract is no longer valid. But that does not mean that commercial pressures won't force you to reduce your prices.

Why is There Only Talk of Prices Having to be Cut? Are There No Opportunities for me to Increase Them?

The reason for this is simple. Any pressure to cut prices is of more concern to businesses than price rises. After all, price cuts can put you out of business. The other factor to take into account is the strong value of Sterling.

Trade has already come under immense pressure as a result of this and as the UK will not join the single currency until at least 2002, and probably as late as 2005 (if at all), British businesses could be trading with the same disadvantages they have today. Only once Sterling starts to drop will these pressures ease. But if the euro is a weak currency, Sterling may rise even further, compounding the problems.

So, Can I Benefit From Adopting the Euro?

Yes, if you trade – import or export – with several euro-zone based companies or countries because it will reduce exchange rate risks. You will then only have to hedge against the euro – a cheaper option than hedging against several currencies.

You can also open one euro account (either with a UK bank or a European one) and avoid suffering exchange rate costs by asking all your suppliers to pay in euros to your euro account. If you make heavy use of European bank transactions the savings could be substantial. If you then needed to exchange balances in your euro account into Sterling, this could be done as a one-off transaction amalgamating several smaller payments, and you can shop around for the best exchange deal.

If and when the UK adopts the euro there will probably be no or very low charges for switching currency from euros to Sterling so the savings will then be far greater. Although converting to euros will be expensive, large companies have looked at the costs and expect to recoup them relatively quickly. For example, Siemens expects transition to the euro to cost about DM100 million but predicts it will pay for itself in three years with annual savings of DM35 million.

When Could Single Pricing Start?

Dual pricing will start from 1 January 1999. Even those pan-European corporations that are adopting the euro for their accounts will still have to sell goods in local currency as consumers will not have any euro currency until 2002.

So, single pricing will not start until 2002. For UK companies, dual pricing will not officially start until we join EMU – although many companies will come under pressure to price in euros as well as Sterling before then. We will then have a transitional dual currency phase before adopting the euro once Sterling no longer exists. If this happens it will not be until 2004 or 2005 at the earliest.

When Will I Have to Start Displaying Euro Prices?

If you are trading with European companies you will probably want to consider changing brochures and price lists shortly after the introduction of the euro in 1999.

As far as consumers are concerned you will not have to display dual prices – both Sterling and euro prices – until after 2002 when the actual currency is introduced. Even then only retailers in tourist areas – mainly the ones who already accept foreign currency – are likely to accept the euro. The remainder of UK firms can wait until the UK joins EMU.

Can I Start Using Euros from 1999 – I Think it Will be a Great Way to Boost Trade in Europe?

If you walked into some Continental hypermarkets in northern France in the Spring of 1998 you would have found goods already marked in euros as well as French francs, even though the actual values were a slight guess. These shops were doing exactly what you want to do – using the euro as a marketing gimmick.

Although euro-pricing for consumer goods will probably take much longer to be adopted than euro-pricing for corporations and financial markets, companies should not become complacent. Increasing consumerism means that companies keeping prices at different levels in different markets will probably suffer. Conversely, those companies that quickly adopt euros and adjust prices to euro-friendly round numbers will gain.

In practical terms it will be far easier to buy goods from the outer reaches of the euro-zone. And that does not just include cheap alcohol or cigarettes. More than 12 per cent of all Europeans purchased clothing in another European country last year. Some 4 per cent bought TVs, cars or washing machines. The cheapness of internet shopping, Eurostar travel and freight delivery means Euro-shopping is increasingly easy.

So I Don't Even Have to be Based in Europe to Gain?

European shopping online is soaring. At just $100 million last year, it is expected to soar to $3.5 billion by 2001 according to research company Datamonitor.

You can also sell via mail order provided the cost of postage or despatch still means your customers save money – or get access to quality British goods they cannot buy in their own country.

But When I Convert my Prices Into Euros, I Get an Unwieldy Figure. I Can't Quote That as my Price.

Although EMU rules require national currencies to convert into euros to six relevant digits, they will be rounded to two significant digits.

That Doesn't Equate to a Consumer-friendly Figure – Can't I Adopt a Different Exchange Rate?

No. Once the UK joins EMU we will be bound by strict rules on conversion.

To get a more consumer-friendly figure – like the euro equivalent of £9.99 or £149 – you will have to adjust your Sterling prices to give a round euro figure. You cannot use a different exchange rate just because the figures don't suit. This will not be a concern initially unless your competitors adopt euro-friendly pricing from 1999.

The other option is to adopt the approach of many pan-European companies. Simply sell goods at different prices (either Sterling or euro prices) to different countries.

So I Can Get Round This by Charging More in Some Countries Than Others?

Yes. For example, car manufacturers charge widely different prices for cars across Europe. One recent survey by the EU found that a Ford Fiesta and a VW Golf cost 40 per cent more in the UK than in the cheapest European country.

However, this may be less of an option in the future because the EU is looking into these pricing differentials. In January 1998 the Commission fined Volkswagen £66 million for not allowing Italian car dealers to sell to customers in Austria and Germany where VW cars cost 30 per cent more. The exemption, which allows car manufacturers to choose the dealers they sell through, comes up for renewal in 2002. However, even before then cross-border competition and possibly the internet will have already had an impact on prices.

In the US internet companies enable customers to shop around for the cheapest cars, order them and arrange finance without leaving their computer terminal. Although harmonization of prices could lead to them being increased in some countries, for British drivers this is unlikely as we already pay more than most other European motorists for the same vehicles.

Convergence of prices in some other product areas has already happened. Expert International, an association of more than 3,000 electrical retailers, says manufacturers' prices diverged by as much as 35 per cent in the early 1990s. Today they are broadly comparable throughout continental Europe.

But What if I Want One Euro Price and Want That to be a Customer-friendly Figure? Will I Then Have to Cut my Prices?

Probably – unless your prices are already competitive.

A survey of corporate finance directors by KPMG Management Consulting in the Autumn of 1997 found that almost half expected EMU to lead to lower prices. However, much will depend on what your competitors decide to do. If the majority plan to round up to the nearest full euro figure, you can probably do the same. The fear is that if all businesses decide to use the euro as an excuse to raise prices, inflationary pressures will be introduced to the new euro-economy. This could destabilize EMU as low inflation/low interest rates are the key to its success.

But What About my Profits?

You don't have to sacrifice profits – just give customers less for less money. Retailers across Europe are already working on what will become the new psychologically-important price points that appeal to customers. Most retailers are expected to round prices down to the nearest full euro figure. Then they will work out what they can afford to give for this price and either reduce the size of the product or launch new ones with higher margins.

Consumer groups are lobbying for legislation to prevent such back-door price increases. However, so far the European Commission has decided that statutory regulation will be too expensive. Instead, it is proposing voluntary guidelines.

5 *Banking*

How is the Single Currency Likely to Affect my Banking Relationships?

It could save you a lot of money if you have different accounts in different currencies. If you can amalgamate a number of foreign currency accounts into one, it will save you a lot of hassle; it will also help cash flow because you will have to keep less money on deposit to keep all your accounts in the black. It should also reduce your bank(s) charges because you will have fewer accounts.

However, if you currently only have a Sterling account and need to open an additional euro account because firms you trade with adopt the euro, you could face increased banking costs. A euro account may not be necessary if you only handle a few euro payments. You could use a foreign currency exchange service or simply ask your bank to convert amounts from euros before paying them into your account. However, as the UK moves towards membership of EMU, euro accounts will become increasingly necessary for more and more businesses.

The fact that banks will only have to handle cash-less euro transactions until hard currency is introduced in 2002 could lead to the following changes:

■ reduced currency conversion costs – although this may not happen immediately

■ faster payment clearing times across European borders

■ different ways of raising cash – a move to more fixed-rate borrowing rather than variable overdrafts

■ if you can amalgamate a number of European currency accounts into one euro account, you may find you need to use less banks; again this will help you to keep the lid on your costs

▌ you're also likely to see new systems being introduced to cope with cash-less transactions. For example there's been much talk of pre-paid spending cards being introduced. This will be particularly useful for people who spend a good deal of time travelling throughout Europe.

Will my Bank be Ready to Deal With Euros From January 1999?

Yes. Several of the major banks have already announced that they will be offering euro accounts and some have even opened them for large customers. Ask your bank what preparations it has made for offering new accounts and services to deal with the euro. Most banks have prepared information and guides on the introduction of the euro so it's worth taking a look at these to see what will be helpful to you.

At an industry level, the UK clearing banks have been working with APACS (The Association for Payment Clearing Services) to improve the UK inter-bank payments infrastructure to accommodate the euro.

How Should I Treat the Euro From 1 January 1999?

For purely banking and financial purposes – as any other foreign currency. So if you currently hedge against exchange rate risks, you should continue to do so. However, if you're planning to make euro payments from currency accounts that are denominated in a euro-zone country you won't need to worry about exchange rate risk – each EMU member's currency will be pegged to the euro from next year.

This means that if you're trading predominantly with Eire, it may be worth having a euro account to cut down the need for hedging each transaction, which can become pricey.

Will I be Able to Have a Euro Bank Account and Cheque Book From Next Year?

Yes, but the clearing cycle for euro cheques has yet to be announced. The major banks have already started to launch euro accounts, which will give customers access to the full range of business banking services.

By the time the single currency is introduced in January 1999 euro banking services will include deposit and euro lending facilities, access to new euro payment channels, euro cash management tools and all other banking products needed for international trade.

If I am Invoiced in Euros, Will I be Able to Make Euro Payments From 1 January 1999?

Yes, from next year you can make all cash-less transactions in euros, so you can write cheques, wire money, etc in the new euro anywhere in the world, including in the UK.

Banks will offer services to enable you to do this either electronically or through manual request forms, which should be available in your local branch.

How Much Will it Cost?

In countries that join the EMU, European banks have promised not to charge their customers extra for converting domestic currencies into the euro. Instead of having a margin – the difference between the buying and selling price of currency – exchange will be at the official rates. However, usual banking charges will still apply. Once euro notes and coins are introduced, a charge is likely to be made for converting these.

Unfortunately the same will not apply to UK banks. British businesses are likely to face the same transaction costs as they currently do for all foreign currency. Small business euro accounts will probably have comparable charges to Sterling accounts.

Until the euro is introduced, accounts can be opened in ECUs and converted to euros. NatWest has said that its euro account will initially be just another foreign currency account for UK customers.

What Happens When Payments Have to be Made Between One Country and Another on a Day When There is a National Holiday in One of Those Countries?

Within Europe there are about 50 days when it is a public holiday in at least one member country. This makes for a long holiday if it delays payments and transactions.

To overcome this potential hazard, the European Monetary Institute (EMI) which will be replaced by the ECB on January 1999, has declared that its inter-bank payment system (TARGET), will be open every weekday except on Christmas and New Year's day.

The UK equivalent is CHAPS (Clearing House Automated Payment System); within Europe CHAPS is referred to as the local RTGS system (Real Time Gross Settlement system). Each country has its own home equivalent to RTGS and, in the UK, for CHAPS to stay open on bank holidays will require a change to English law. If the law isn't changed and you are expecting payment on a bank holiday, you may have to send it via another country where the RTGS system is open.

Re-routing a payment may also have complications; some contracts may not allow you the freedom to re-direct payments without the prior agreement of all the involved parties.

Until Euro Notes and Coins are Introduced How Will Payments be Made?

Most payments will be electronic although cheques can also be issued. The absence of euro cash will further encourage the shift away from notes and coins to electronic payment methods.

Credit and debit cards will be the main method of euro transactions for consumers. There will also be greater opportunities to pay by corporate and purchasing cards for businesses. As a result Visa has predicted that spending on cards could triple over the next three to five years.

Stored value cards – or electronic purses as they are known – will also be pushed. Currently Mondex and Visa Cash are the main electronic purses and there are some 100 million of the cards circulating in Europe although currently they only work in the country of issuance. Once the euro is introduced they will become cross-border payment cards.

When Will I Have to Start Banking Euro Cash?

Widescale use of euro cash will not start until the transitional period when the euro will be able to be used in the UK as a parallel currency alongside Sterling. This is unlikely before 2005 although use of the euro in the UK may well spread in the run-up to EMU entry.

It is less likely that the use of the euro will spread much to the retail sector while the UK remains 'out', according to the Bank of England. However, it states that it is 'likely' to be used in some high street retail stores, particularly in tourist areas, like Oxford Street in London, and in some card transactions, so the euro will be used in much the same way as foreign currencies are at the moment. And, from the beginning of 2002 euro banknotes will be brought into the UK by tourists and other travellers.

Exchange rate 'spreads' – the difference between the buying and selling price of currency – are to be charged by banks, bureaux de change and retailers when switching euros to Sterling and most will also charge a handling fee on top. As such this will probably restrict the use of the euro, just as it restricts the use of foreign currency.

But once the UK commits to join EMU it will be bound by currency conversion rules; this means that there will be no 'spread' on conversion. Although you could still be hit for handling fees, the increased competition is likely to mean these fees will be kept to a minimum.

I Don't do Any Business Outside the UK so Why Should I Need to Consider Having a Euro Account?

If you supply a company that does a lot of business in Europe, it may decide to switch to using euros. If such a company converts all its business into euros it'll be able to reduce its risk to currency exposure, particularly now, while the pound is so strong.

If this happens, it's more than likely that the company you supply will start paying you in euros. So even if you've never had to deal with foreign currency transactions before, you may well have to start doing so now.

Who Will Need a Euro Account?

Anyone paying or receiving payments from other European companies but also from EU organizations.

Even farmers could receive their EU subsidy cheques in euros as from 1999. The advantage of this would be that farmers could use these euro cheques to buy fertilizers or pesticides or even tractors from multinational producers in the euro-zone. This means they won't have to worry about exchange rate fluctuations between Sterling and the euro which will make it easier to budget for the future.

But as we said earlier in this chapter, it is not only the EU that will be paying in euros. Large companies are also adopting the euro as their accounting currency. In turn this will affect SMEs. 'Suppliers of financial services may face demand for the euro sooner rather than later in Stage 3 (the transitional period) from small or medium-sized companies affected by the requirements of large corporations adopting the euro from the start,' warns Lloyds Bank.

Will I Have to Have a Euro Account to Make Payments in Euros?

No, but if you think you're going to be using the euro for a number of transactions, particularly if you're going to be receiving a lot of payments in euros, it's worth considering because you'll be able to cut down on the number of conversions you have to make between the euro and Sterling.

What Happens if, Say, my German Supplier Starts Invoicing me in Euros Instead of Deutschmarks; Can I Still Use my Deutschmark Account to Pay Them?

Yes, until 2002. From next year the deutschmark will become a denomination of the euro, so provided you have enough money to cover the euro invoice in your account, you can pay it from your deutschmark account.

Again, if you have trading relationships with a number of different European companies in different countries, it's worth reviewing the number of foreign currency accounts you have. It could be a lot cheaper if you close them in favour of just one euro account.

So Should I Start Thinking About Opening a Euro Account now, Even Though the Euro Will Not Replace Local Currencies in the 11 EMU Member States until 2002?

This will depend on the companies you trade with – and not just those in the 11 'in' states.

Although the Bank of England expects the euro to be used by many UK-based companies which trade across the Single European Market, and by companies from the euro area trading with the UK, other companies could be affected. But you should not wait until 2002 to make this decision because the euro will be a trading currency from 1999. For example, German giant Siemens has indicated that it intends to introduce the euro as the official company currency in their subsidiaries outside the euro area on 1 October 1999.

However, again as we said earlier, just because you are paid in euros does not necessarily mean you will need a euro account. You will be able to pay in euro amounts to Sterling accounts as you do today with all foreign currency payments.

So Who Will be Opening These New Euro Accounts?

Most banks anticipate the biggest demand from the corporate sector. Euro products and services will be ready by 1999 for these larger firms even though the UK will stay outside the EMU. NatWest says:

> We believe that there will be early and extensive demand for euro services in this segment. For retail banking in the UK, entry into EMU is the critical factor. We do not believe that there would be strong demand for euro services from most personal and small business customers until towards the end of any transitional period.

When Can I Open One?

Some accounts have been opened already by banks for high-profile corporations. But by 1999 all banks will be offering them to customers.

Surely This is Just Another Way for the Banks to Charge me Even More. How Much will it Cost me to Convert Into Euros?

Member States joining the single currency in the first wave will adopt Commission recommendations on payments. These state that banks should not charge:

▌ for conversion of incoming and outgoing payments denominated in euros or the national currency during the transitional period

▌ for converting accounts from the national currency to the euro either during or at the end of the transitional period.

But This Will Not Affect Us in the UK?

True. But there will be pressure on banks to keep costs to a minimum. And remember it is not just the exchange costs that have to be taken into account. The spread – the difference between the buying and selling price of a currency – can be as much as 5 per cent.

Because the euro will be such a big currency and once the UK is 'in' banks will have to exchange money at par, they will probably keep this spread to the minimum.

What Will my Bank Statements Show?

Bank accounts probably won't show euro and Sterling amounts. For a start, rounding could mean that the total figures do not tally. Instead your euro account will be entirely in euros.

However, if you pay in a euro deposit to a Sterling account – or vice versa – the euro amount will probably be shown on the statement as a memorandum item. That is what happens currently when you use your credit card abroad. The foreign currency amount is shown but a Sterling amount is added to your credit card balance.

So the Rounding of Figures Means Sterling and Euro Totals Will Not Tally?

This has not been finalized but the British Bankers Association, the banks, BACS and APACS have been looking at this issue and have recommended that amounts should be converted and rounded to meet the Maastricht Treaty's Article 235 Regulations. Generally six significant figures will be used by banks when converting to and from euros but they will then be rounded to two decimal places. This means they will not always be rounded in the customer's favour.

What? So I Could Lose Money Purely Because Conversions will be Rounded Up or Down?

In the long run you will win some and lose some, so no – only those who pay in large amounts of small sums which all convert to euros will lose money.

For example, if you were to pay in 10,000 different amounts of 100.0049 euros you could really suffer because when converted to Sterling, each payment may equate to 100.00. This is an exaggerated example – and highly unlikely as you would generally pool all your payments and pay them in as 1,000,049 euros so would not suffer any rounding problems – but it gives you the general gist of how it could work. It means the difference in the Sterling value of a large number of small payments and one large payment could be quite significant.

The Bank of England states 'the differences might sometimes be substantial. BACS is planning to undertake a simulation to assess the total financial effect and the possibility of redistributing any large differences is being considered.' But this problem will only be an issue for banks and very large companies. Most SMEs will find that the rounding means they win in some cases and lose in others.

Another alternative may be to price goods at euros 100.0055 rather than 100.0044 so you win rather than lose in the conversion process.

How Will my Accounting Software Cope if my Bank Rounds to a Different Figure to the One I Have Calculated?

If the payment is made by BACS, the original euro amount may not be shown if your account is credited with a Sterling amount. This could make it hard for your automatic reconciliation software to match payments. However, this problem is likely to be solved well before it becomes an issue. APACS and the Business Accounting Software Developers' Association and Computer Services and Software Association are working together to find a solution.

Once European Banking Systems are Integrated, Will I Find That Payments are Faster?

It can currently take up to 25 days for a cheque to be processed through the European banking system. Compare this to the low-cost, same-day, cross-border payments with no exchange costs promised by the introduction of the euro.

For SMEs this scenario is still some way off. Work to enhance the UK inter-bank payments infrastructure to accommodate the euro is being coordinated by APACS. The aim is to ensure the basic infrastructure is in place to handle euro payments.

BACS is planning to develop a second clearing stream to handle euro transactions during the transitional phase when the UK will be using a dual currency. This will be similar to the current clearing system – not real time.

But I Heard That the New TARGET System Would be Real Time?

TARGET is the Trans-European Automated Real-Time Gross-Settlement Express Transfer system. It will – as its name implies – offer real-time transfers of money.

Access for the UK will be via CHAPS euro. However, as far as businesses are concerned it will not apply. It will primarily be used for monetary policy purposes and wholesale transactions. And use of TARGET may be restricted by the European Central Bank because we are an 'out' country. However, CHAPS euro will have access to 5,000 banks across the EU through TARGET. There is likely to be a fee for this service and for businesses clearance will not be same-day.

So What Systems Will Business Use?

SWIFT is currently the most common method of making cross-border payments. However, the time taken for payments to reach your account or to be received by those you are paying varies.

In future the system currently used for clearing ECU, the Euro Banking Association (EBA) Clearing system will become the main clearer of euros. More than 50 major European and UK banks have already joined this clearing system and membership is growing. From 1 January 1999, this system will provide same-day value payments and net end-of-day settlement with settlement taking place at the European Central Bank after the introduction of EMU.

In this sense, the euro is not just another currency – it will be a means of improving the efficiency of cross-border payments.

Are There any Other Methods of Cross-border Payments?

Yes, IBOS (Inter Bank On-Line System) – this is based on an association with eight European banks in the UK, France, Spain, Portugal, Belgium, Italy, The Netherlands and Denmark. It's mainly used by corporate customers as a cash management system enabling customers to make same-day value payments and receive same-day information from accounts with banks in the association.

What are the Main Benefits of Using These Electronic Payment Systems?

▌ The cut-off times will be longer, so you can request payments later in the day.

In time, same-day value payments should be guaranteed but only for institutional and corporate transactions. Eventually smaller firms should also benefit from faster transactions.

What About Bank Charges? Will They go Down in Future?

Purely in practical terms, bank charges will eventually have to be converted into euros. So they could rise or fall if they do not convert into a clean round number.

The Bank of England has suggested altering Sterling bank charge tariffs so they convert to convenient, round euro amounts. Whether this leads to an increase in bank charges remains to be seen.

The advantage of a euro account will be that euro transactions will be at no extra cost. Some banks have already committed to allowing customers to keep existing account numbers when converting to euros.

In terms of the pricing policy of banks, that tends to be dictated by competitive pressures. If more European banks muscle in on UK business that could lead to a reduction in charges.

What Will the Euro Look Like?

The design for the euro banknotes has been chosen by the EMI Council (European Monetary Institute). It chose the theme of 'Ages and Styles of Europe'.

There will be seven euro bank note denominations (5, 10, 20, 50, 100, 200 and 500). The notes feature windows, gateways and bridges from the seven ages of Europe's cultural history. There will be eight coins, and they'll be denominated in 1, 2, 5, 10, 20 and 50 cents coins; there will also be a 1 euro and a 2 euro coin. Each coin will have a national mark on one side, but the notes will have no national identification on them at all. So although the notes will be identical the coins will not. However, Britain has said that it wants to keep open the option of putting a national symbol such as the Queen's head on one side of its notes if it joins EMU.

If Britain Joins the Single Currency, Will Scotland and Northern Ireland Still be Able to Have Their Own Notes?

This will be a decision for the ECB. In theory the Maastricht Treaty does allow these countries to retain their own national notes, but they may not be considered to be legal tender if Britain joins.

What Will Happen in the Channel Isles and the Isle of Man?

These countries have a monetary union with the UK but they're not part of the EU. It's unlikely they'll decide to join the EU but if Britain joins EMU they may decide to switch to using euro notes and coins so that they can continue their monetary links with the UK.

How Will the Bank Clearing System Deal With Euros From 1999?

CHAPS will run two clearing systems in parallel – one for Sterling and one for the euro. This means that customers will be able to make same-day value euro payments within the UK even while Britain is out of EMU.

If and when we decide it's time to join, CHAPS will immediately switch to settling inter-bank payments in euros only, although customers will retain the option to choose which currency they want to settle in until the transition period runs out.

As of March 1998, six major banks had signalled their intent to join the CHAPS euro service from its inauguration in January 1999 and many others are expected to join from April 1999.

Initially the CHAPS euro service expects to handle only 15,000 items a day although substantial growth is anticipated after 1999.

If I Have to Pay or Receive a Cheque in Euros From 1 January 1999, How Will the Banking System Handle It?

Euro-denominated cheques drawn on foreign banks will be returned to the bank on which they are drawn for payment – as they are today.

If Britain Decides to Join EMU What Will Happen to my Sterling Loans?

Most loans will just be converted into euros when this happens, but don't miss this as an opportunity to review your borrowing requirements.

Can my Bank Force Me to Switch my Loans Into Euros While Britain Stays out of EMU?

No, and even if Britain joins EMU in the future, which means that further down the road your loans would be converted to euros, the bank has no right to cancel existing loan agreements or to adapt the terms of your loan using EMU as the excuse.

And if Britain Does Join EMU, How Will it Affect my Outstanding Loans?

Your loan will be re-denominated into euros, so will the interest, but the interest rates on fixed-rate loans will remain the same. Only floating rate loans will be adjusted, as they would be today, for any change in interest rates.

Will Sterling Exchange Rates be Fixed Against the Euro From January 1999?

No, because we're not going to be in the first wave of EMU entrants. Only those countries joining EMU next year will have the exchange rates fixed to the euro from next year. And, at the moment, the Government has ruled out joining ERM2 (the new Exchange Rate Mechanism).

So, every time you carry out a payment in euros from your Sterling account, you'll be affected by the current exchange rate and you'll probably be charged a fee for the conversion.

Is There a Chance I Might Have Euro Cash in my Pocket From Next January?

No, notes and coins in euros won't come into circulation for another three years (2002). If Britain is still 'out' of EMU at this time, the euros in circulation will be treated just like any other foreign currency, although Marks & Spencer, for example, has said that from October 1999 it will install new tills that will be able to take euros and the dollar. If Britain decides to join EMU it will probably go through a transition period like the rest of Europe to give us time to phase out Sterling and replace it with the euro, so don't panic.

Will I be Able to Open a Bank Account With a European Bank Instead of a British Bank?

You already can. However, you will not have the same access to services as if you had an account with a domestic bank. Strategic alliances between banks may give you more options. If a UK bank has a link with, say, a French bank you will be able to use the branches of that bank in France as if they were branches of your own bank. This should cut costs and make banking easier.

6 *Accounting for the Euro*

The main accounting change for businesses is the way currencies are converted from January 1999.

What if I am Asked to Trade in Euros Before My Systems are Modified? Are There Any Legal Requirements I Must Know About?

In theory, if you already trade in more than one currency you can simply add another currency – the euro – to your accounting packages or calculate the figures manually. But you must meet the legal requirements set down in Article 235 covering conversion between 'in' currencies. This sets out how conversion between denominations will be made and how rounding procedures should be applied.

So What do the Regulations Require Me to Do?

Transactions between the euro and its national denominations must be based on the same official exchange rate, i.e. 1 euro = 6.60054 French francs. However, inverse exchange rates (1 mark = 0.X euro) are not allowed. This could cause a problem if your accounting systems are not geared up to cope with this conversion procedure.

So every system that carries out any form of currency processing must be reviewed and currency conversion algorithm routines modified where necessary. If you have bought a multi-currency software package (rather than developing your own) the software manufacturer should be able to advise you as to whether your system needs modification and if so how to upgrade your system.

How is the Calculation Done?

When converting from euros to national denominations of euros you must divide the local currency total by the conversion factor – for example, 1000 DM ÷ 1.97048 which gives euros 507.49056067. According to the Bank of England you cannot multiply by an inverse rate such as an approximation to the reciprocal of 1.97048 like 0.507491, as for large sums the use of inverse rates would produce inaccurate results.

Are There Any Other Problems I Need to Know About?

In addition to the currency algorithm some systems may have to be modified to cope with the decimal places of the euro and rounding up and down. For example, Italy, Belgium, Spain and Portugal only use whole numbers in their national currencies. Because of the decimal places in the euro, systems will have to allow for up to six positions for decimals.

The Bank of England states that when you are converting from national denominations of the euro into euros you cannot round figures. All conversions must be to six significant figures. So if you are converting 40.6684 Belgian francs into euros you cannot do the calculation assuming 41, 40.7 or 40.67. However, if you are converting from Sterling or US dollars into euros there is no convention about how amounts should be rounded.

So Will I Have to Pay in Fractions of Euros?

No. Although calculations can be done using up to six decimal places, all figures must be either rounded up or down to two decimals. Your system will have to cope with this.

So Which Way are Figures Rounded?

If the result is exactly half way, round up. Below half way round down, and above half way round up.

I Have Heard the Term 'Triangulation'. What Does That Mean?

What it means is this: there will be no direct exchange rates between national currencies of those countries that have adopted the euro. All national currency units will be expressed as a sub-denomination of the euro. By law, conversion between them must be through conversion into and out of the euro. So, for example, francs must be converted to euros (by division by the conversion rate) and then that euro figure must be converted into deutschmarks (by multiplication by the conversion rate). This is a requirement because the decimal places vary from currency to currency. Sterling has two decimal places but the lira none.

However, triangulation will not affect Sterling until we join EMU. So trades between France and the UK, for example, will still be directly from one currency to the other.

Even within the triangulation calculation there are strict rules on rounding and the result of the first calculation (as in the example above, from francs to euros) can be rounded but to no less than three decimal places.

So How Will it Affect Me – After All the UK Will Not Join EMU in 1999?

If you only trade with one European country it will not affect you. However, if you have, for example, a subsidiary in France that trades with another 'in' country, those transactions will have to follow the triangulation rules. So, only if you have transactions between 'in' countries will your accounting systems be affected.

However, even if you are trading with only one 'in' country and in Sterling you may still want to covert via the euro – a similar process to triangulation although the rounding processes are slightly different. Businesses opting for this can then get used to dealing in euros in preparation for the day when the UK joins EMU. The Bank of England has warned that this may cause difficulties for some computer software packages and advises businesses to avoid confusion by making clear which method has been used.

It also warns that it could be argued that using cross-rates – rather than converting via the euro – could be in breach of Article 235 because there is an implicit exchange rate with the euro which may be different from the explicit exchange rate. However, the opinion is that there would be no breach of Article 235.

How Do I Go About Assessing My Accountancy Needs?

Your accountant should be able to give advice particularly on any gains/losses arising from converting/translating EMU currencies to the euro. You should also assess your needs for dual accounting and, if you will have to accept euros as well as Sterling, review all your accounting systems to ensure they can cope with debt, orders, invoicing, payments, historical data, etc. Check with your accounting software supplier that any consolidation packages can be used in both euro and non-EMU currencies.

What Are The Main Pitfalls I Should Watch Out For?

Complying with the currency conversion and rounding rules should be relatively straightforward if you have the right software (see Chapter 7). The biggest threat to your business will be from errors and fraud. Errors can occur if, for example, 100 deutschmarks are entered into your system as 100 euros. At the same time you could be vulnerable to fraud during the confusion.

Will I Be Able to Write Off the Costs of Meeting the Requirements of the Euro?

As with any other business expense, the costs can be claimed as expenses – or capital allowances if new equipment needs to be purchased.

7 Information Technology Issues

The introduction of the single currency is not just a political and economic issue; it is also a major information technology problem. Coming so soon after the expense of the Millennium bug problem, changes to accounting, pricing, marketing and retail systems to cope with the new currency represent another major expense.

The shortage of IT staff – already stretched dealing with Millennium problems – means that many firms will have to postpone any work on adapting systems to cope with the euro until nearer its introduction. This may not be a bad thing. For a start, many firms are reluctant to spend time and money on new IT systems when it is still uncertain when – or even if – the UK will join the single currency. So businesses that have already assessed the impact of the euro and found that they will now have to invoice, pay or accept payments in euros do have some time before adapting their systems. But they should not be complacent. The UK could join EMU in as little as five years' time. So firms should at least start planning how they will adapt if only to save the expense of paying for new systems in the next year or so which will then have to be replaced again between 2002 and 2005.

The situation is far more urgent for businesses already trading in Europe. They may not only find that they are at a competitive disadvantage if they do not adapt their systems by 1999 but could also lose business.

I Am Only Just Sorting Out My Millennium Bug Problems. Why Do I Have to go to Even More Expense to Adapt my IT Systems to the Euro? After all, the UK May Not Even Join

If you do not trade with other European companies, do not go to the expense of making your systems euro-compatible just yet. As the UK will not join until after 2002 at the very earliest you do have a few more years to decide what action to take.

However, if you do trade with Europe you are likely to find you come under pressure to trade in euros over the next few years and so will have to modify your systems. How else are you going to cope with conversions which must be to the correct number of decimal places and calculate the correct rounding of figures?

Remember, IT problems often take longer to solve than you allow for. So even if you are not planning to do any changes until 2002, you will have to start preparing for these changes now.

So I May Have to Upgrade All My Systems Again in Just a Few Years' Time?

Yes. So bear this in mind when renewing any IT products or even cash tills and vending machines. If you expect your systems to last more than five years you could be in for some extra expense. However, if you expect to be replacing any systems in 2002 to 2005 you can simply upgrade to euro-compatible systems at the same time.

Which Computer Systems Will be Affected?

Accountancy and financial software initially. Any software that issues invoices and processes purchase orders and/or sales orders in euros or deals with payments in euros.

Can I Cut IT Costs by Upgrading my Existing Systems, or Do I Have to Buy New Ones?

Most software companies are making any necessary changes to their packages to cope with the euro. However, you will have to pay for new software. You may also have to modify hardware as you will not have the correct keys for the euro symbol.

What Software Will be Euro-compatible?

The new Windows 98 software will incorporate the euro symbol. Alternatively Microsoft has a free service package which it will make available through its website – www.microsoft.com – which will solve problems for users of Windows 95 and Windows NT4. However, this will only help if you use one of the three most popular typefaces. So if you do not have an internet connection or are a user of Windows 3.11 you will have to pay to upgrade your software.

Other software companies have developed products that will upgrade Windows 3.11, Windows 95 and Windows NT4 so that they include the euro character set.

I Already Have a Multi-currency Accounting System, So Why do I Need to Upgrade?

As explained earlier in this chapter, the euro will not be just another currency. It will be an alternative way of expressing each national currency of the Member States participating in the euro. This is because the exchange rates will be fixed for these countries on 1 January 1999.

So instead of converting from deutschmarks to francs you will have to convert from DMs to euros and then from euros to Ffr. Your accountancy software will probably not be able to cope with this as inverse exchange rates between the euro and national currency units are not allowed (national currencies must be converted to 1 euro, not the other way round).

In addition, as we approach membership of the single currency your system will have to cope with dual currency – transactions in Sterling and euros. This will mean that all business transactions will have to be recorded in both national currency and euros.

You may also have to handle payments in a currency different to that on the document/invoice. Once we join the single currency there will be no legal difference between Sterling and euros. So a Sterling invoice can – at that time – be paid in euros or vice versa. Accounting software will not only have to accept these payments but also cope if the payments are in a different currency to that on the invoice and have a device to check that the payments match.

The system will also have to handle triangulation – the fact that there will be no direct exchange rates between national currency units of 'in' states. As the UK already has two decimal places in its currency the other systems issue – the fact that currency conversions are to six significant figures and must show data to two decimals – should not be a problem.

So How Do I Know if Software is Compatible?

Your existing systems will probably not be compatible as packages are not tailored for the fixed conversion factors to six significant figures or the special conversion and rounding conventions.

If you are buying a new package the Business and Accounting Software Developers' Association, BASDA, has published a specification for producing software systems that can cope with transactions involving the euro currency. In future, it will certify systems as capable of handling the task.

Will I Have to Meet These Requirements Even Before the UK Joins the Single Currency?

At the most basic level, you may have to add the euro symbol to keyboards and adapt software packages. This may have to be done even if we don't join the single currency as you may come under pressure to price, invoice or pay in euros.

So How Much Will This Cost Me?

IT consultants the Gartner Group have estimated that the total cost of adjusting software will top US$100 billion. And it warns that there may not be enough IT specialists to carry out these software adjustments in time. However, as the UK will not be joining the single currency until at least three years after the first wave, UK companies should be able to take advantage of the work done in other European countries.

As far as SMEs are concerned, the costs should be relatively small. Most software vendors claim their software programs are, or will be, euro-compatible.

So, is the Euro Basically an Accounting System Issue?

Initially it will be. But the costs will not end there. Once the euro is introduced as a hard currency, tills and vending machines will also be affected.

But I Don't Have to Worry About Handling Currency Yet?

No. But you will after the year 2002 (or whenever the UK joins EMU). In business terms that is not far off. If you deal in large amounts of cash you may also need new machines for counting, weighing and measuring the new currency.

So I Face Even Further Expense?

Yes. And for some firms this will outstrip the costs of modifying IT systems. Most estimates put the cost of adopting the euro at 1 to 2 per cent of retailers' annual turnover although small shops will face proportionately higher costs.

What Hardware Will be Affected?

Credit card and debit card terminals, tills and vending machines. However, credit card companies will simply add the euro to their list of currencies so there will be minimal disruption. Changes to tills and vending machines will not happen for several years, until the euro is issued as a hard currency on 1 January 2002.

Tills will have to be adapted to cope with both Sterling and euros once we are in the dual currency phase. Even then there is no urgency. It is only when – and if – Sterling no longer exists as a hard currency that all coin-operated machines will have to switch to euros.

Since most tills have a life of around five years, retailers need to plan their timing now, or they may find that they need to replace tills that they have only recently bought.

So I Will Have to Adapt Systems to Cope with Two Currencies and Then Adapt Them Again to Cope With One?

That is up to you and the type of business you run. But generally the answer is yes.

During the transitional phase two currencies will be in circulation. The transitional phase will not even begin in the UK until 2002 at the very earliest. In the countries in Europe that join the single currency on 1 January 1999, this will be between 1 January and 30 June 2002. So during this time retailers will probably have to accept both currencies unless they opt for a 'big bang' approach and switch from one to the other overnight. Most tills are not capable of handling two currencies so they will have to be adapted to cope. Then once local currencies are withdrawn from 30 June 2002 they will have to accept only euros. The exact timings for this changeover in the UK have yet to be decided.

If you are a retailer you will have to prepare for the following:

▌ how you are going to convert and round prices to meet the required regulations

▌ how your tills will cope with two currencies – the till software will need to show the euro and Sterling prices although this may be as a total rather than for each item

▌ what your till displays will show – will they show prices in Sterling and euros?

▌ how your bar-coding and scanning equipment will handle the conversion

▌ the possibility of your needing new tills to cope with two currencies

▌ whether, during the dual currency circulation phase, you will give change only in Sterling or in both Sterling and euros

▌ how you are going to train staff to cope.

Will I Have to Make All These Changes?

No. The Commission's expert group on this issue is promoting a flexible approach to dual displays – so you will not have to pay for expensive modifications of existing equipment or new equipment just for the dual currency period. Dual display can be limited to the final price to be paid by consumers. The group has made four proposals for those wanting to adopt dual pricing, including retailers, utility companies, banks and insurance companies. These are:

1. fixed conversion rates should be used when calculating counter values in dual displays
2. a dual display should not place an obligation on the retailer to accept payments in euros
3. there should be a clear distinction between the lead unit in which the price is set, and the counter value which is displayed for information purposes only
4. voluntary agreements on common formats or design of dual displays should be encouraged.

It is likely that these proposals will form a 'standard of good practice'. Regulation is seen as a last resort and will only be proposed if voluntary codes of practice prove ineffective.

What is the Best Way to Prepare for These Changes?

Don't look at them as just IT problems – think about your business strategy as well. According to Richard Heinzer, head of the Year 2000/Euro Project Group of the Winterthur Group:

> Before IT people can get to work, they need to know where they are going. In other words, the business strategy is the prerequisite for the technological changeover. In addition, the introduction of the euro is a more complex problem in that whole systems will have to be changed, and not only certain specific aspects. In addition, we have to be able to convert every local currency into the euro.
>
> Unlike the euro, the lira, the escudo, the peseta and the Belgian franc do not have decimals. Even when we have come up with a solution for one country, we cannot treat it as a model solution and simply apply it to any other corporate unit.

What Should I Ask my IT Suppliers?

First, are they going to adapt their products to cope with EMU? If so, when? How much will upgrades cost and what will they entail? For example, will the systems be modified to handle dual currencies (for the stage when Sterling and euro notes and coins are in dual circulation) or will they just be able to cope with the new conversion rules?

You will be charged for these upgrades. Unlike the Year 2000 changes, the single currency is a new requirement.

Can I Use Technology to Help me?

Yes. You will find the internet one of the biggest sources of information. There are several sites that deal mainly with information technology; they are:

http://www.ispo.ce.be/yzkeuro
http://www.ispo.cec.be/yzkeuro/src/wdiseuro.htm (information
from the European Commission)
http://www.xs4all.nl/~doornh/euro/BAR.HTM (A Dutch development institute specializing in euro and Year 2000 conversion
solutions)
or try the Microsoft web site – http: ///www.microsoft.com and
do a search for 'euro' and select the downloads for the operating
system you are using
computer consultants CMG's site – http: //www.cmgplc.com –
also has some useful information on computers, software and
the single currency.

Any Other Useful Contacts?

The British Computer Society has published a booklet, *Preparing
for the euro.* It costs £10 for BSC members and £15 for non-members.
Contact 01793 417 417.

8 Currency and Interest Rate Risk

You may need to consider hedging against currency fluctuations for the first time if UK companies you deal with decide to adopt the euro. This is because fluctuations between Sterling and the euro could wipe out any profits if the currency's value changes between agreeing a price and receiving payment.

If you already trade overseas you will know how expensive hedging against currency movements can be for small businesses. Whether or not you decide to hedge your currency, you should still be aware of the risks your business faces.

Why is the Issue of Exchange Rates Such a Crucial One?

British businesses are already painfully aware that the high value of Sterling has pushed prices to uncompetitive levels. So the impact of EMU on exchange rates is key to future business planning – not only for those who trade in Europe but also companies which operate solely in the domestic market and which could be priced out of business by cheap imports.

Every UK business is – and will be – affected by the value of Sterling and exchange rates, regardless of whether or not they export or import goods, because they have an indirect effect on interest rates. While Sterling remains strong, there is the added problem of having to deal with cheap imports from our competitors. All in all, it's not a happy situation.

Any businesses failing to prepare for fluctuations in the value of Sterling on the assumption that joining EMU will be 'years away', could be in for a rude awakening as some economists are predicting a roller-coaster ride for the pound over the next few years.

Is Sterling Now Likely to Fall in Value? My Exports Have Been Severely Hit Already

In the long term it is hoped the answer to this question is yes. However, there are fears that if the ECB sets a low interest rate for euro-land from January 1999 – and the euro is a 'soft' currency – Sterling will rise even further. There are two factors behind this. If the UK has higher interest rates than the rest of Europe, investing in Sterling becomes more attractive. Fears that the euro may be weak are also prompting investors to look to stronger currencies like Sterling (particularly if British interest rates are higher than in the euro-zone) because they will get higher returns on their investments. This could be bad news for the British economy and will be disastrous for British exports.

What are the Costs of Exchange Rate Risks to Business?

It's difficult to quantify this because the markets are volatile and change daily, but the scrapping of foreign exchange and hedging costs within the euro-zone will save European companies vast amounts when they adopt the euro. Daimler Benz alone estimates it will save $55 million a year, which equates to a massive $65 billion pan-European saving. Unfortunately the UK won't see any significant benefits unless individual companies doing most of their business in Europe use the euro as their main currency. While European companies can trade in the certainty that exchange rates will not work against them, UK businesses will continue to be hampered by uncertainty while at the same time paying higher transaction and currency conversion costs than their rivals in EMU Member States.

It's therefore inevitable that some UK companies will come under pressure to price their goods in euros as well as Sterling but at the same time they'll be at a competitive disadvantage when it comes to the overheads associated with currency conversion.

With the Advent of the Euro, Will Foreign Exchange and Interest Rate Hedging Still be Relevant?

Yes, particularly while Britain stays 'out' of EMU. The basic hedging principles will still apply, particularly if your base currency is Sterling. The reason for this is that the euro will 'float' against the pound, the dollar and all other non-EMU member countries so the foreign exchange risk you currently experience in dealing with foreign currencies will remain.

But What About Interest Rate Hedging; Aren't European Interest Rates Going to be Fixed by the ECB?

No, the ECB won't be fixing interest rates; it sets them, rather like the Bank of England sets British interest rates. Therefore, euro-zone interest rates will move up and down over time, so you can't afford to be complacent and if European interest rates are likely to affect your business, you should consider hedging against your interest rate exposure too.

What Will Determine the Interest Rates Set by the ECB?

The rate at which interest rates are set by the ECB will very much depend on the economic situation at the time. The ECB will want to make sure inflation is under control and that monetary policy is running smoothly. The setting of interest rates will be one of the ECB's strongest weapons to keep the euro-zone economy in check – rather like the Bank of England uses interest rates to control the UK economy.

It is expected that euro-zone interest rates will be lower than ours because the money and capital market rates of the new EMU member countries are already very close and converging strongly with Germany's. But, if something goes hideously wrong and EMU becomes unstable, this theory goes out of the window.

If I Want to Start Hedging my Interest Rate and Foreign Exchange Exposure in Preparation for the Euro, Can I do it Now?

Yes, you can, because until January 1999 the ECU will remain so you can take out positions against the ECU. After January 1999, the ECU will be converted on a one-for-one basis against the euro, so they become one and the same.

Will the Single Currency Reduce my Hedging Costs?

Absolutely, but by how much depends on how much foreign business you do. However, eliminating 11 currencies and replacing them with one should mean you can make a substantial saving.

Within the Euro-zone Interest Rates are Likely to be Lower Than in Britain. How is This Likely to Impact on my Interest Rate Management?

This poses two key questions that you should consider. First, as a long-term borrower, should you fix any or all of the interest rates on your borrowings now? Second, if interest rates are likely to come down further, should you wait and bear the brunt of short-term rates constantly changing?

If you choose the first option, fixing your rates now, this could prove to be more expensive in the long term but will reduce your exposure to interest rate volatility. If you go for the second and take the heat, you could offset some of the risk by hedging.

9 Borrowing, Grants and Raising Finance

How Could EMU Affect Britain's Borrowing Climate if We're Not Members?

Britain's economy has been plagued by yo-yoing interest rates. They affect the cost of borrowing and the value of Sterling. This makes it extremely difficult to write long-term business plans to project future earnings for any British-based company. High interest rates have already damaged many UK exporters, pushing Sterling to record highs which have made British goods uncompetitive.

EMU could save us in this respect. We're already greatly influenced by the European economy, but with EMU we will become more so. And, if Gordon Brown, the Chancellor of the Exchequer, pursues his policy of making sure we're prepared to join EMU when the time is right both politically and economically, we will become even more tied in to following the European model of low interest rates and low inflation. As a result, this period of preparation by the Government should be very good news for Britain's businesses, particularly when it comes to borrowing money and writing business plans.

You also need to note one other significant development – the removal of exchange rate risk is likely to lead to the freer movement of capital throughout the euro-zone as institutional and private investors look to diversify their investment portfolios to take advantage of the opportunities that will arise from EMU. This will create new opportunities for much smaller companies to look at raising money via the capital markets rather than via their banks.

This will create new opportunities for businesses that in the past wouldn't have dreamt of raising money through the capital markets. In fact, British Steel recently issued its first-ever bond to finance expansion plans. In future much smaller companies will have access to these bond markets. It's a very exciting new development and will create a mass of new opportunities for entrepreneurs and expanding businesses. Some economists are predicting that such a shift in corporate funding will completely change the corporate climate of Europe.

But How Will the Euro Affect my Outstanding Loans?

It won't, unless you wish to convert them into euros. Even if Britain joins EMU in the future, which means that further down the road your loans would be converted to euros, your bank has no right to cancel existing loan agreements or to adapt the terms of your loan using EMU as the excuse.

And if Britain Does Join EMU, How Will it Affect my Outstanding Loans?

Your loan will be re-denominated into euros, as will the interest, but the interest rates on fixed-rate loans will remain the same. Only floating-rate loans will be adjusted, as they would be today, for any change in interest rates.

If Interest Rates are so Much Cheaper in the Rest of Europe, Can't I Take Advantage of This?

Only if you borrow from a bank in Europe. Interest rates, set by the European Central Bank, are currently just 3.5 per cent. So borrowing costs are far cheaper. But to borrow from a Continental bank you will need to have business interests in that country and assets to borrow against. Also remember that interest rates are not the only factor. Exchange rate fluctuations could cost you dearly. Unless you switch all your trading to euros you will be affected by rises and falls in Sterling. So if Sterling falls by 10 per cent, you will need 10 per cent more Sterling to repay your loan. This currency risk could easily wipe out any interest rate savings.

What About European Union Finance and Grants? If We Are Not Members of EMU Will British Businesses Still Be Able to Get These?

Yes, and these are already available for British companies to take up.

They include the European Technology Facility for investing in venture capital funds supporting high growth and technology-oriented SMEs in the EU. The European Investment Bank venture capital scheme is being run by several venture capital companies in the UK. GLE Development Capital is involved in one of the funds. Baring Private Equity Partners with its parent ING and the European Investment Bank will run the largest – a £120 million fund for the English regions. Advent will be running the second largest, a £100 million fund, aimed at start-up and early-stage high-tech firms especially in healthcare and information technology. An additional £20 million is being raised by Midland Bank and the EIB to support a network of Midland enterprise funds. Details of these funds and copies of a new guide for businesses seeking venture capital are available from the British Venture Capital Association, Tel: 0171 240 3846.

In addition UK firms can get financial backing to set up joint ventures with other European companies. In the UK this Joint European Venture programme is being managed by Greater London Enterprise on behalf of the European Commission. Firms must have a turnover of less than £40 million and fewer than 250 employees. The investment in a joint venture must be 'substantial' – an investment of at least 15 to 20 per cent of the total costs of the joint venture project. To qualify, businesses must show the venture will create new jobs, not just shift them from one country to another.

These are just two of the European-backed schemes to help small and growing businesses. For more details on others contact your local Business Link.

What About EU Subsidies?

These may be paid in euros from 1999. They are already denominated in ECUs so there will be no change to the amount paid – just how it is paid. Instead of subsidies being converted into each country's own currency through the agrimonetary system of 'green' exchange rates, subsidies will be in euros.

What Will Happen to Regional Aid?

Many smaller companies indirectly benefit from regional aid as it encourages larger employers to move into an area and in turn to use the services of local businesses. If your firm is based in an area which benefits from the £1.5 billion of EU funds given to Britain's regions, it is essential that you monitor what the EU is proposing. In addition your region may qualify for aid for the first time, attracting extra potential customers for your business.

The Alliance for Regional Aid has tried to quantify the impact of the EC's draft plans for 2000–2007. It says that seven parts of Britain may qualify for aid: Cleveland, Tyne & Wear, Merseyside, South Yorkshire, Greater London, West Midlands and the Isle of Wight. However, regions and rural areas may lose out because their unemployment level is below the EU average.

10 *Taxes and VAT Issues*

British businesses currently enjoy such low taxes that the UK is regarded as a tax haven by many corporations. Therefore any change to this tax status is likely to cause concern.

The creation of euro-land with a powerful federal government will inevitably mean some tax harmonization – if only so that individual member states can compete on a more equal footing. Germany's finance minister, Theo Waigel, already has a vision – which has been backed by France and Italy – that this will mean the end of competing tax rates. This threatened lack of sovereignty in levying taxes, combined with the loss of Member States' rights to set interest rates, is one of the political stumbling blocks to Britain joining the single currency. It is inevitable that any loss of power in determining taxes, interest rates and laws will lead to a political backlash.

Waigel is not alone. Mario Monti, the EU Commissioner responsible for tax matters, has also indicated a desire to introduce a single EU tax system – although he has not gone as far as saying it openly.

However, even if harmonization of taxation is not enforced, rates of taxation are bound to converge due to market pressures. Single tax rates, while creating what Waigel says is a 'perfect' single market, are not essential. The USA is not threatened by differences in state taxes. The sales tax in Oregon is 0 per cent and in New York is 8 per cent, yet that does not mean everyone in New York flies to Oregon to shop.

Any attempt to introduce single taxes is likely to meet massive political opposition. Member States will have already lost the right to determine interest rates and exchange rates, leaving taxation one of the few economic weapons still under the control of individual country governments which are unlikely to allow any further erosion of their power.

At the March 1998 meeting of EU finance ministers in York it became clear that after EMU tax policy will no longer be an exclusively national affair. However, this may not necessarily be a bad thing for business. One of the issues discussed at the meeting was venture capital, which is undeveloped compared to the US. One way for governments to encourage economic growth was seen as using special tax breaks to encourage venture capital.

This was only one aspect of the harmonization of taxes discussed. A reflection of this convergence of tax rates was given in the 1998 budget which contained elements which brought the UK more in line with its European partners.

Will EMU Mean UK Businesses Pay More Tax?

Britain's corporation tax rate is 21 per cent for small businesses and 31 per cent for corporations – the lowest in the EU. It means UK firms have a competitive advantage against, for example, German businesses which must pay 57 per cent tax.

So any tax harmonization will inevitably mean that UK tax will have to be raised – not cut. However, as tax rates are not currently on the EU agenda, increases are unlikely. The threat to tax rates could come once the UK joins the EMU and loses the power to determine interest and exchange rates. It will mean that the only means of stifling an overheating economy may be taxation.

Surely This Will Help UK Businesses?

The UK attracts 45 per cent of the EU's entire inward investment mainly as a result of its favourable tax regime but also because of language, incentives and political goodwill. So while we may have higher labour costs than some of the southern European Member States, the UK will still attract major employers. This in turn will help the SMEs which trade with them.

So the UK Can Attract Trade by Keeping Tax Rates Low?

In theory, yes. However, the EU has been looking into a voluntary code of conduct to prevent 'unfair' tax competition from disrupting the Single Market. So when – and if – we join, the EU could try to put pressure on local tax rates. However, this is unlikely. Ireland, with a 10 per cent corporate tax rate until 2010 for manufacturing and traded services, has told the Commission that interfering in the setting of national rates is beyond its remit.

What Will Happen to VAT Rates?

The 15 EU nations have more than 2,000 different VAT rates. These range from levies on cars of 15 per cent in Germany to 213 per cent in Denmark. Again, a unified VAT rate has not been proposed. However, the European Commission is considering a draft directive on the harmonization of the VAT system across the EU.

Will This Mean a Single VAT Rate?

No. The proposals, scheduled for implementation by 2001, are largely technical. The main change is that they will require VAT to be charged at the rate applicable in the supplier's country.

How Does This Change the Current Rules?

Currently, if you are trading with other EU Member States and both businesses are registered for VAT, the seller zero rates goods and services and the buyer pays VAT at his country's rate on the supply and then treats this as input tax. If you sell goods to an unregistered EU business you simply add UK VAT in the normal way. In future, instead of supplies being charged at the UK rate and treated as input tax, VAT will now be charged at the rate in the country of supply.

Accountants Argue That This Origin-based VAT System Will Immediately Make Full-blown VAT Harmonization Necessary. Why?

Companies will inevitably want to reduce the amount of tax they pay. So they will relocate their country of VAT registration to countries with lower VAT rates.

What Other VAT Rules do I Need to Know About?

If you are VAT registered you have the right to reclaim VAT incurred on services abroad in all EU countries. However, many companies fail to reclaim the full amount. This is partly because of the red tape involved and the need to fill in application forms in the local language. So for small amounts, particularly VAT on business travel and expenses, many businesses find it's not worth the bother. Some companies, such as Cash Back, will do the work for you.

What Are the Different Standard European VAT Rates?

Austria	20%	Italy	20%
Belgium	21%	Luxembourg	15%
Denmark	25%	The Netherlands	17.5%
Finland	22%	Norway	23%
France	20.6%	Portugal	17%
Germany	15%	Spain	16%
Greece	18%	Sweden	25%
Hungary	25%	Switzerland	6.5%
Iceland	24.5%	UK	17.5%
Ireland	21%		

Will I Have to Pay my Tax in Euros?

No, not until the UK adopts the single currency. However, companies can (subject to certain conditions) elect for corporation tax to be computed on the basis of accounts drawn up in a foreign currency such as the euro, and the self-employed as well as individuals will also be able to pay their taxes in euros. VAT can also be paid in euros. The Inland Revenue should make payments in euros as easy as any other foreign currency.

What if I Have Accounts Drawn Up in a Currency That Will be Replaced by the Euro?

The Government is planning to introduce legislation to convert automatically an existing election for a currency which joins EMU into an election for the euro.

Will This Conversion Lead to a Tax Charge?

It shouldn't. If a tax charge would not otherwise have arisen, re-denomination into euros should not affect your tax position.

Will the Conversion of a Contract From a European Currency Into Euros be Regarded as Crystallizing a Taxable Gain?

No, it shouldn't. However, this has yet to be clarified by the Inland Revenue so you should ask your accountant or tax office for advice.

Will the EU Scrap Tax Havens?

Tax havens are seen as an 'obstacle to the European Single Market'. As such there is a fear that Europe's tax havens could lose their special status.

This is seen as a further step towards bringing the tax-raising powers of all EU states under Commission control. Although the EU is a potential threat, there are no firm plans that will lead to the ending of tax haven status for Luxembourg or Andorra. The Channel Islands will not be affected as they are not EU members.

11 Legal Issues and Regulation

The introduction of the EMU is, as we have already said, going to involve much more than just another currency. It is going to affect your decisions about which currency you want to trade in, whether or not you want to change your existing contracts and, if you have a publicly quoted company, whether or not you re-denominate your share capital.

EMU will also make European unification irreversible and lead it further down the road to a federal Europe which in turn will mean more Euro-legislation, regulation and red tape. This will mean more power for the EU in dictating how we run our economy and businesses. The Social Chapter and the minimum wage and the raft of other Euro-laws already introduced are just the start.

While it is easy to get carried away debating the pros and cons of EMU, there are some pressing issues which we need to start dealing with right now – not least of which is how the single currency will affect both existing and future contracts. If you have not thought about this, you should – particularly if you're dealing with a company that is likely to start using the euro as its main trading currency in the next few years.

From January 1999 the financial details of any contract that is held with a company or country in the euro-zone will be read as if it were in euros even if the wording used is, say, French francs, because the franc will be fixed against the euro. Similarly if the contract refers to ECUs, from next year the ECUs will be automatically substituted with euros.

There is also legal provision to ensure that someone cannot use the introduction of the euro to discharge or excuse the performance of any legal obligation – this is designed to stop someone from trying to unilaterally alter or terminate an existing contract. And there are regulations to allow you to pay or receive payment in either euros or one of the euro-zone currencies for the next three years (until 2002); again, the euro-zone currencies will be fixed against the euro.

In Theory Then You Could Argue the Euro is not Going to Alter the Term of Any Legal Instrument, so What's the Big Deal, Particularly if Britain is not Going to Join EMU For at Least Another Three to Five Years?

Whether Britain joins EMU or not, a number of companies which trade in Europe, and that includes Eire, will switch to using the euro as their main trading currency because they will find it financially expedient to do so. It will reduce their currency risk exposure, put them on a more level playing field with their European competitors, etc. As a result they will be reviewing their contracts with their suppliers and their customers to reprice them in euros. The domino effect will begin yet again: if a company has switched to using the euro as its main trading currency, that company is going to find it very tiresome if it has to deal with a handful of British-based suppliers who still want to be invoiced/paid in Sterling. So the pressure will be on for companies further down the chain to start using the euro instead of Sterling.

I Already Receive Grants in ECU From the EU. How Will These be Affected by the Euro?

The ECU is a basket of all the European currencies, including those of Britain, Denmark, Sweden and Greece, none of which is going to join EMU in the first wave. On 1 January 1999, the ECU will be replaced by the euro at a rate of one for one. If you have a contract that is expressed in 'official' ECUs, you will find they are replaced automatically with euros at the rate that is set at the close of business on 31 December 1998 as laid out under the terms of the Maastricht Treaty.

Will Britain be Affected by the New Single Currency Laws, Rules and Regulations?

Yes, if you are a company that trades with EMU member countries or companies, or you are a subsidiary of an EMU member country company.

How Will this Affect Contractual Issues?

Technically, existing contracts won't be affected by the introduction of EMU under the concept of 'continuity of contracts'. This means that contracting parties cannot terminate or alter any existing contracts as a consequence of the single currency. This basically stops anyone trying to use EMU as an excuse to improve the terms of an existing contract in their favour. This is covered within Article 235 Regulation enforced from 20 June 1997. It states that:

> The introduction of the euro shall not have the effect of altering any term of a legal instrument or of discharging or excusing performance under any legal instrument, nor give a party the right unilaterally to alter or terminate such an instrument. This provision is subject to anything which the parties may have agreed.

This also means that if a fixed rate of interest on a transaction has been set prior to the introduction of the euro, it cannot be changed.

So, in summary, the euro will not provide any party with an opportunity to wriggle out of any contractual arrangements that were agreed to prior to 1 January 1999.

Will the Continuity of Contracts Law be Fool-proof For All Contracts?

Unfortunately not. Although the EU law provides for automatic contract continuity, it does not deal with issues arising from the economic or commercial consequences of the introduction of the euro which, a party may argue, take effect to 'frustrate' a contract.

So, if one party does not want automatic contract continuity they may find an opportunity to wriggle out of it if, for example, adopting the single currency is going to cost them more money. While EU law respects the principle of freedom of contract, one party can make specific provisions for matters that arise as a result of the introduction of the single currency.

In other words, one party could try to make the other responsible for the costs associated with converting to the euro, although there is a phrase, 'no compulsion, no prohibition', which will apply between 1 January 1999 and 2002.

What Does 'No Compulsion, No Prohibition' Mean?

This is a clause to protect you. During the three year transition period that has been set by the Community to physically switch to using the euro, you can keep your options open as to which currency you want to use without any obligations – that is, up until the year 2002 – and you cannot be forced to use euros if you do not want to. In reality this is meaningless: if your business is involved in buying widgets from France and you wish to pay in francs you can do so, but the franc's exchange rate will be set against the euro, so in effect you will be paying the same rate either way and taking the same foreign exchange trading risk in both currencies.

Really the only advantage it offers you is the opportunity to run your bank account in euros from the UK. The UK has said it will not be joining ERM2, which will peg non-EMU member currencies to the euro, but if you are trading with euro-land most of your business will be in euros as a result. It may therefore pay you to switch to euros yourself.

If you decide that this is the best way to minimize your exposure to currency risk and it is easier for your business, then you can also file your accounts in euros if you meet certain criteria set out by the Inland Revenue. However, if you do this, you will, until Britain joins EMU, still be faced with actually having to pay your tax bill in Sterling or paying the Inland Revenue to exchange it. You will also have to pick up the tab for the currency risk exposure.

Nonetheless if the bulk of your business involves exporting to EMU-land, it may be to your advantage to take up this option and switch to using the euro as your main trading currency. Conversely, if you are a buyer of EMU-land products, and the pound remains strong, you would probably be better off sticking to Sterling. You should seek professional advice before making a final decision on this issue, particularly as Sterling could be in for a bit of a rocky ride when EMU is introduced.

A contractual obligation to pay an amount in, say, French francs will, from 1 January 1999, become an obligation in the French franc denomination of the euro. It will have to be discharged by payments denominated in the franc unless both parties agree otherwise. However, if you have agreed to pay in euros after 1999, then you will be obliged to do so, unless of course both parties agree otherwise. In effect, for what it is worth, you won't be forced to trade in euros unless you want to – 'no compulsion, no prohibition'.

What if One of my Business Partners Wants to Use Euros and I Don't?

Legally, you won't have to, but, at the end of the day, it will boil down to business clout. If your partner wants to use euros and you don't, it could be a question of finding another partner, giving in or, if you are the stronger of the two in your relationship, forcing the issue.

What Happens Then if I Have a Contract Requiring Me to Pay in, Say, French Francs After 1999? Will I Have to Pay in Euros or in French Francs?

If your existing contract stipulates payment in a particular currency, payment should continue in that currency during the transition period, ie until 1 January 2002, unless all the parties involved agree to change the payment terms.

If I Decide to Accept or Make a Payment in Euros Instead of French Francs, How Will This Affect My Bank Account?

Your bank, assuming it is in Britain or within euro-land, will be required to make the conversion and to credit or debit your account in the same currency in which your account is denominated; in the case of British companies it is likely to be Sterling. Your bank will then automatically convert the currency you have used for your deal at the fixed conversion rate regardless of where the payer or the receiver is based.

But, if the contract is governed by English law, payment in euros will be recognized by an English court only if it is a valid discharge of debt under the law of the place where the debt has to be paid. So, if for example you accepted payment of a French franc debt in euros into your British account, unless both parties agreed to it being paid in euros, you would be better to insist that payment is made in French francs until you change the contract.

So, Going Back to the 'No Compulsion, No Prohibition' Clause, Could I be Forced to Accept Payment in Euros After 1 January 1999?

No, but your contract might have been drawn up in such a way as to enable the paying party to pay in euros, in which case you would have to accept payment in euros. You will have to make your own decision on which currency you wish to use. As the euro is expected to become the most widely used foreign currency in this country for foreign-based transactions, other than the dollar, it's an important decision and one you should take time to consider.

Does This Mean That Existing Contracts Won't Automatically be Re-denominated if They are with a Company in a Participating Member State after 1 January 1999?

Yes, but only during the transitional period. So, until 2002, the obligation will continue to be denominated in the national currency unless you and your counter-party agree to re-denominate it into euros.

How Will This Affect the Netting of Cross-claims if I Switch to Using Euros?

Netting and set off will remain unchanged and the normal obligations that apply to monetary transactions will remain the same during the transition period irrespective of which currency is used.

How will Contracts That Have Been Made With Non-EU Member States be Affected?

EU regulation only applies to those countries which are members of it, so contracts made under non-EU law but concerning EU currencies will need to contain specific clauses to deal with the introduction of the euro.

In some areas such as New York, legislation has already been introduced to provide (in general) for the automatic continuity of contracts following the introduction of the euro but you will need to take advice on this issue depending on the contracts you have and which currency you intend to use.

What Will Happen on 1 January 1999 to Contracts That Are Subject to EU Law but Which Are in a Non-EMU Currency?

Nothing, unless the EU country in which the organization with which you have such a contract is based decides to join EMU. This would happen if, for example, you have a contract with a Danish company and Denmark decides to join the second wave of entrants.

What Type of Contracts Will be Affected by All This?

Every contract you have with a company that decides to adopt the single currency will be affected – that means life assurance policies, derivatives, swaps, distribution agreements, employment contracts, service agreements – practically everything and anything which can last beyond the end of this year!

So, Does That Mean Every Contract Will be Affected and if I Want to Contest it I Can Fall Back on EU Regulation to Protect Me?

Alas no – each contract will have to be looked at in isolation because the law is not clear on what amounts to an agreement which is outside the regulation. In other words, if one party claimed that the existing contract can be frustrated by the 'economic and commercial consequences' that would arise from sticking to it, the other party could have legal grounds to extricate themselves from the existing contract.

What Sort of Issues Should I be Thinking About Before Making Any Future Decisions on Both Existing and New Contracts as a Result of the Single Currency?

You will need to make a checklist with which to review and assess both existing and future contractual arrangements and how they may be affected after both 1999 and 2002. You need to consider:

▊ Will monetary amounts be replaced by the euro?

▊ Are your pricing sources/benchmarks going to change?

▊ Will existing obligations be changed?

▊ Will it be necessary for you to change existing contracts?

▊ Will EMU create an environment for force majeure to be applied to your existing contracts?

▊ In which currency will you denominate new contracts?

▊ Do you need to insert a continuity clause into existing and new contracts?

▊ How will the euro affect the price of existing fixed rate agreements, force majeure, interest rates?

▊ If the euro imposes additional costs, who will bear them? For example, if you convert to pricing in euros and you find that you have to round down, how will you allocate the losses you will inevitably incur? If, for example, you export an item of clothing and the retailer wants to change the euro price from euro 13.45 to a more consumer-friendly figure of euro 12.99, you may have to look at who bears this loss or possibly at reducing the quality of your product. With products that are in pack sizes – for example a box of 45 chocolates – you may decide to agree with your customer that you reduce the amount given: for example, the box may have to contain three fewer chocolates to make up the price difference. This in turn will have implications on packaging and manufacturing.

Earlier in the Book You Talk About the Maastricht Treaty. How Will This Become National Law?

The Treaty provided the blueprint for the creation of a single currency. The actual timetable and detail of EMU were worked out afterwards, most notably at the Madrid Summit at the end of 1995 and the Dublin Summit at the end of 1996.

All the decisions made at these summits had then to be transformed into law via secondary legislation which was made under the treaty. Technically, unless Britain decides to join EMU, we will not be affected by it but, in order to keep the door open for us to join should we want to after the next election, as announced by Gordon Brown, the Chancellor, in 1997, we will find the economy is being run so that we do comply with the requirements of the Maastricht Treaty. Gordon Brown needs to bring down the level of Government spending, borrowing and interest rates to make sure our economy is in line with the rest of Europe.

How Will the Changeover be Regulated?

The new European Central Bank will be the key regulator of EMU. It will decide whether new countries which wish to join EMU are eligible and it will have the right to impose financial penalties on countries which bust the convergence criteria. This means that if for example one country borrows more than it should, the ECB can penalize it. Technically, there are two pieces of legislation that will regulate the changeover to a single currency. One is based on Article 235 of the Treaty of Rome and the other on Article 1091(4), which was inserted into the Treaty of Rome by the Maastricht Treaty. The introduction of EMU was done as a set of rules that were created by 'Regulation' rather than as a 'Directive'. The reason for this is that when rules are laid out as a Regulation there is no room for interpretation, which means that no one can bend the rules to suit their own local needs. A Directive, which is effectively a form of secondary legislation, has to be ratified by local law before it becomes legal – this leaves room for loose interpretation of the law.

So Will These 'Regulations' Affect Us in the UK?

Yes and no. The reason for this is that the 'Regulation' has had to be divided into two parts because the Council underestimated the need to agree certain requirements such as how to treat ECU-denominated obligations after 1 January 1999 in order to enable financial institutions enough time to get their houses in order to cope with the transition to a single currency.

Originally it was thought that EMU could be introduced under a single article in the Treaty – that was the Article 109l(4) which was inserted into the Treaty of Rome by the Maastricht Treaty. The Maastricht Treaty envisaged a straightforward process for the introduction of the single currency. It soon became apparent that switching from the basket of ECU currencies to a single currency (the euro) was going to be very complicated and fraught with both technical and political difficulties.

In order to get the legislation passed under Article 109l(4), participating Member States have to vote on it. However, they could not vote on it until the initial 11 members were named in May, and the process of voting takes at least six months. That would be too late for them to be able to get everything through in time to meet the deadline of 1 January 1999 set by the current timetable.

So Britain has been affected by the first part of the regulation concerning continuity of contracts and the treatment of ECU-denominated obligations but not by the regulation laid out in Article 109l(4) which will now be passed by the 11 member countries. This regulation will introduce monetary law to enable member countries to switch their national currency into euros. Britain is not involved in this part of the regulation because of the legal opt-out it negotiated, along with Denmark, at Maastricht, but it is involved in the second aspect of the regulation.

What is the Second Aspect of the Regulation?

There is an Article in the Treaty called Article 235 which allows for legislation to be passed in order to attain 'one of the objectives of the Community' as an emergency facility if the provisions made to give the Treaty enough power to get EMU off the ground prove insufficient. It is known as the 'sweep up' provision. The Community had to go back to this provision because it encountered a vigorous attack from the financial community.

The financial markets needed legislative certainty on key issues, such as the protection for existing contracts and the treatment of ECU-denominated obligations well before membership by the 11 initial participating countries states was confirmed. (If it had not been given this, the introduction of the euro next January would have created havoc in the financial markets.) This was achieved via Article 235 Regulation which came into force on 20 June 1997.

Does Article 235 Regulation Affect Britain?

Yes, it does. It affects all of Europe's 15 Member States and deals with continuity of contractual obligations and the treatment of ECU-denominated obligations after 1 January 1999. It also sets out the mechanics that apply when converting currencies into euros.

The purpose of this 'sweep up' legislation is to try and ease the transition period for the banks and other financial institutions when it comes to what has been called the 'big bang weekend'. This is the New Year weekend, 31 December to 4 January, that the banks have to convert all their positions and their clients' positions to run alongside the euro. It involves a huge amount of work and a great deal of money, so they needed all the help they could get.

The second regulation based on Article 109l(4) can finally be enacted now that the 11 Member States for the first wave of members joining next year have voted. This is effectively the monetary law of the Member States participating in the single currency and deals with the changeover from national currencies. That is why it does not, at this time, affect Britain.

What about EU Regulations – How Will They Be Affected by EMU and Will There Be More Red Tape For My Business?

EU regulations will affect British businesses whether we join EMU or not. Although new EU directives are not being introduced as part of EMU, they do go hand-in-hand as part of the Commission's plans to create a more level playing field for trade.

So What New European Directives Could Impact on my Business?

If you take advantage of increased cross-border shopping and sell to Continental consumers either directly, through mail order or over the internet, the new consumer guarantees directive will affect you. At the time of writing, the government had not yet responded to the taskforce that is looking into this issue, but it is expected that this directive will also be adopted for companies selling goods in the UK. The directive moves the burden of proof regarding faulty goods from the buyer to the retailer and manufacturer. The law will give shoppers the right to return goods and have them repaired or replaced within two years of purchase. However, they will have to return the goods to the country where they bought them.

What About Imperial Measurements – Aren't They Going to be Banned?

The metric system has already been adopted for most packaged goods, although the old imperial weights and measures are usually displayed alongside. However, the EU has proposed to ban the use of imperial measurements entirely at the end of 1999.

The taskforce looking into this has asked for this time period to be increased so that both types of measurements can be used after

1999. It is also looking into other weights and measures legislation and has recommended a repeal of all legislation prescribing quantities that is not required by the EU, to simplify the whole system.

If your business is – or could be – affected by any of these new regulations it is essential that you keep yourself abreast of any changes. The sooner you are aware of any potential additional costs to your business, the more time you will have to prepare.

12 **Employment Issues**

As you are running your own business, you may not feel that employment issues arising out of EMU will affect you or your company. However, increasing employee rights in the form of the minimum wage, maximum working week and new unfair dismissal procedures will affect every employer, as will wage inflation.

Although employment reform will not be introduced as part of EMU, the Social Chapter and the stability and growth pact are part of the EU's plans to create a more level playing field for trade. More indirect effects on British businesses will be felt if EMU leads to growth putting pressure on wage inflation. Alternatively, once governments can no longer determine economic policy using interest rates to boost growth or increase/decrease the value of currency, individual states run the risk of higher unemployment if the local economy begins to decline. This in turn could lead to higher social security costs and therefore could impact on taxation.

The other threat is that firms you work with will relocate to countries in Europe with the lowest employment costs. Although it is hard for workforces to move from country to country, it is relatively easy for companies to do so. This is exactly what happened in the US where American companies moved jobs from high-cost cities to cheaper ones, or to Mexico.

A recent report in *Business Week* estimated that one in five workers will be disrupted by mergers and downsizing and some 5 per cent of industrial workers could lose their jobs. More than 11 per cent of the euro-zone's workforce is unemployed, but the level varies widely from country to country. In Member States where it is highest there will be less pressure on wages. But in countries like the UK with relatively low levels of unemployment, high wage demands remain a threat. The worrying increase in wage levels led to the 0.25 per cent increase in base rates in early June 1998.

Although UK unemployment is low, this may not be the case for much longer. Former trade and industry secretary Margaret Beckett warned that, 'The euro will expose very clearly those companies which are genuinely competitive, efficient and cost-effective and those which are not.' The Government says that productivity levels in British firms are up to 40 per cent lower than those of their international rivals and that this gap will be highlighted by the euro.

Multinationals including car manufacturers have already indicated they will begin pay negotiations in euros. This in turn will lead to greater wage/productivity transparency, making it easier for firms to compare salary levels across the EU. Although this will not affect small businesses in the UK directly, if major companies you supply decide to relocate you could find that you lose lucrative contracts.

How Will the Euro Affect Pay?

The euro will make it far easier for executives to compare salary, taxes, take-home pay and living costs across European countries. So those working for pan-European companies will be able to put more pressure on their employers to standardize remuneration.

Most workers will not migrate across borders in search of the highest wages, but that will not stop them putting pressure on employers for pay parity with other European countries. However, the threat of job losses if employers decide to relocate to low-cost economies should dampen this pressure.

I've Heard People Talking About the 'Social Chapter' as Something That's Closely Entwined With the Maastricht Treaty. What is it?

The Social Chapter is the section of the Maastricht Treat that deals with employment rights. The UK negotiated an opt-out, but we are adopting much of what it contains. The minimum wage of £3.60 an hour will be introduced in April 1999. A maximum working week of 48 hours per week has just been introduced.

In addition, the Government has proposed more employee rights in its new Fairness at Work White Paper. This could come into effect as early as Spring 1999 and give workers the right to bring an unfair dismissal case against you after working for you for only one year instead of the current two.

Agency workers, home-workers, subcontractors and freelances may also be able to claim for unfair dismissal. Currently if you lose a case at an employment tribunal (formerly known as an industrial tribunal) the maximum award you have to pay is £12,000. In future there may be no maximum limit on the awards given.

By next spring when the new law comes into force, you will have to give employees a right to time off for family emergencies such as looking after a sick child. This is known as compassionate leave. By then you will also have to give all parents the right to three months leave until their child is 8. This is in addition to maternity leave and the compassionate leave requirements. This rule will apply to fathers as well as mothers. The leave can be unpaid. As parents may change jobs during this eight-year period and it could be difficult to keep records of days off, it is likely that the leave will be in the form of an annual allowance.

If you have more than 20 staff and 40 per cent of these vote in favour of union recognition, you will, in future, be obliged to recognize the union for collective bargaining on pay and conditions.

Sounds Like a Lot of Extra Red Tape and Extra Costs For my Business

Although smaller employers will be exempt from some of the new laws, there will be an increasing burden on small employers, particularly from the minimum wage.

These will be in addition to extra employee rights given under existing European Directives and the Treaty of Rome. Employers who fail to understand how these laws could impact on their business could risk large claims for compensation.

Remember, these laws will apply whether or not Britain joins EMU.

Is it All Bad for Business?

No. The 1997 Treaty of Amsterdam set out the promotion of employment as 'a matter of common concern'. It emphasizes the importance of making taxation employment-friendly by cutting non-wage labour costs. More flexible working practices are also being promoted so that employers can offer more adaptable fixed-term contracts which supply some job security but also meet the needs of businesses. If legislation moves in this direction rather than burdening businesses with greater costs, it will in the long run be good for employers.

How Will Labour Costs Affect my Business?

The euro will not only make prices across individual states more transparent, but also labour costs and other overheads. Productivity will also be more easy to assess.

This is likely to lead to larger corporations relocating or basing more of their operations in the lowest-cost countries. For SMEs which supply these firms with everything from stationery and staff to raw materials and marketing, this poses a threat.

13   *Managing Change*

EMU will create a lot of uncertainty and anxiety among your staff, your clients, customers, suppliers and even your service providers. In fact, the French have estimated that it could trigger a 3 to 4 per cent drop in consumption.

Meanwhile, there is evidence that some banks are already assessing corporate customers' credit worthiness on whether or not they are prepared for EMU. The consequences of the impact of EMU could therefore be quite catastrophic for companies who fail to manage the necessary changes.

What are the Key Planning Issues That I Need to Look At?

There are certain principles that have been widely recommended for managing the change process. These vary, but the key points for you to consider are as follows.

▌ Senior managers play an important role in demonstrating their commitment to implementing the necessary changes to your organization. If you're committed, your staff will be too.

▌ Establish a working group to coordinate and communicate the changes that need to be made.

▌ Appoint a project manager to track EMU developments within Europe, their impact on British business, and to lead your in-house developments.

▌ Review the importance of each EU country in relation to your business; you need to do this from both a supply and a sales perspective.

▌ Embark on a thorough analysis of the opportunities and threats that EMU will create for your business.

First, we would suggest you prepare a planning chart. A typical preparation chart for EMU would be in two stages and is shown below.

A PREPARATION CHART FOR EMU

Stage 1

Define your approach	Assess key euro impact areas	Confirm changes to key processes	Develop implementation plans
Tailor the approach to your own organization	*Impact should be assessed from a number of angles: eg business function, processes, timescales and your own analysis of the impact EMU will have on your business*	*Planned changes should be assessed according to strict cost/benefit, those that are necessary versus those that are desirable*	*Prepare details of the tasks, the structure of your resources, time-scales and overall costs involved*

Stage 2 – Implementation

▌ Confirm plans.

▌ Secure resources.

▌ Empower projects.

▌ Apply project management disciplines.

To make a successful transition to EMU and, above all, in order to seize competitive advantage, requires detailed attention, careful planning and total enterprise commitment. Pressure on key resources will be intense as deadlines mount. The project management structure should be cross-functional with a direct report to an EMU project manager. The key will be to manage the process across the organization, to communicate intensively and to build and implement rigorous change plans. Leading companies are already positioning themselves to exploit EMU and smaller companies will soon have to do the same. (Price Waterhouse)

How Should I Structure my Euro Plans?

That really depends on your business and the impact you think the euro will have on your business and the resources you have at your disposal.

If you're thinking about appointing a euro project manager, it should be someone who is already a senior manager or someone who you are prepared to give enough authority to, to be able to deal with the issues that are going to crop up. Ideally your project manager should make a direct report to senior management so decisions can be made and implemented quickly.

The skills you should seek in your project manager really depend on your assessment of how you think EMU will affect your business. If you think it's going to have a greater impact on your company's market positions, the products you sell and the overall strategic position of your business, it would probably be better for your project manager to have experience in sales and marketing. If the euro is more likely to have a technical impact then a senior finance or accounting manager might be better suited to the task.

Once you have a project manager in place, he or she can take responsibility for coordinating your business's efforts within the timetable you have already established. If you already have a project manager dealing with the Millennium issue, these two people should work closely together to capitalize on any over-lap between the two projects; alternatively the same person could assume responsibility for both tasks.

What Are the Next Steps That I Should be Thinking About Taking?

If you think EMU is the catalyst to expand and/or modernize your business, seize this opportunity.

Once you have identified the areas in which you think a single currency will affect your business you'll need to work with your project manager and other departmental heads to coordinate all activity. You need to be sure that everyone knows what your business objectives are and how you plan to meet them within a certain time frame.

Should I be Asking my Managers to Make a Direct Contribution to this Process?

Yes, they should be playing a key role in helping you with future strategy. Some issues you should ask them to consider are:

▮ how the euro is likely to impact their area of the business and,

▮ whether or not a consultancy firm, legal adviser, accountancy firm, marketing and PR firm, etc will need to be hired to help leverage all the opportunities it will present

▮ what threats they think EMU might pose to their department and the overall business

▮ what opportunities they think it will create.

Once they've carried out their own assessment, they should report back to the project leader so that he or she can prepare a full report on what needs to be done so that the changeover process can begin.

What Should be in the Project Manager's Report?

It should contain an indication as to what resources will be needed to manage the process, eg budget, internal and external resources.

It should also contain a timetable with lead times so everyone is fully aware of what they have to achieve and in what time frame.

What Are the Key Objectives my Business Should be Working Towards?

■ Optimizing the opportunities that may be created by EMU and minimizing the threats.

■ Organizing the changeover in the most cost-effective way you can.

■ Using the changeover as an opportunity to review existing systems and seek out new ways of improving efficiency.

How Can I Maintain the Momentum and Support For Such a Project When Everyone's Trying to Deal With Day-to-day Business Pressures at the Same Time?

This is where senior management commitment to the project is critical. By showing your commitment to the process of change and the need for it, you'll inspire the rest of the workforce to work with you in achieving your goal.

You'll also have to monitor the changeover plan. It may be appropriate for the EMU project manager to form a support committee with representatives from each department (assuming you have different departments) or staff responsible for each area of your business. The team must have regular briefing sessions to review progress on all outstanding issues. There should also be regular feedback to senior management so that issues of importance can be dealt with promptly.

Reward people for their efforts, particularly if they're having to work overtime in order to meet their day-to-day responsibilities as well as work on the EMU project team.

The project manager's role must be to maintain the support of key staff. He or she must make sure they are fully briefed on what is going on both with the political and practical implementation of monetary union as well as what decisions are being taken within your own firm.

What are the Main Areas For me to Consider in This Change Management Process?

We've prepared a checklist in Chapter 16; briefly, the main points are to look at what your suppliers are doing, what changes you need to make to your marketing and sales operations, how EMU will impact on your banking and treasury operations, and how it will affect your finance and accounting functions.

Broken down into these four categories, you can look at the individual issues within each category. Some examples are given below.

Suppliers

Which of your suppliers are likely to be affected by the changeover to the euro and what impact this will have on your business? What percentage of your raw material costs are paid for in the currency of the supplier? If you currently settle these costs via bank transfer through a foreign bank account would it be appropriate to change these arrangements? Will you be able to change your hedging methods as a result of EMU and if so how? You also need to look at the issue of contract continuity, which supply contracts will go beyond 2002 and whether your standard supply contracts need to be revised.

Marketing and sales

Which of your customers are likely to be affected by the euro and will you need to review your pricing strategies so that you quote in both Sterling and the euro? This has implications for your catalogues and price lists. If you currently invoice to companies in euro-zone currencies, will you have to start invoicing them in euros to remain competitive? How will you accept payment – euros or Sterling – and will this mean you have to change your hedging methods so that you can receive payment in euros? If you use a factoring or invoice finance company you also need to find out what they propose to do in preparing for the euro. Again you'll need to assess your current contracts, which sales contracts go beyond the EMU timescale, which standard contracts need to be revised and whether you will you need to issue multi-currency priced contracts. Questions to ask yourself also include whether or not you need to change your current arrangements with agents; whether you can you handle dual currency invoicing/statements, and how you plan to communicate with your customers about the impact EMU's going to have on your business.

Banking and currency exchange/risk

While EMU will create opportunities to reduce the number of currencies you have to deal with, British companies will remain at a disadvantage to their euro-zone competitors because they'll still have to convert all euro-based transactions back into Sterling and bear the costs and risks associated with this.

To keep your costs to a minimum, you can look at opening a euro bank account, making payments in euros both here and overseas, and accepting payment in euros. Other things you need to review are whether it's worth making more use of the electronic banking services on offer, and how you manage your cash flow – the single currency could mean you can reduce the number of banks you use and the number of accounts you have to have. If you have subsidiary offices in the euro-zone, you might find ways of streamlining your cash management further. Other issues you need to consider are whether you need to make arrangements with your bank for handling euros on your behalf, and whether you should borrow in euros rather than Sterling.

14

Internal Communications and Training

Why Do I Need to Put Internal Communications on My List of Priorities When There Are so Many Other Important Business Issues That Need to be Dealt With?

Quite simply, because they're crucial. If you don't explain to people within your organization what you're doing and why, they're going to resent the extra work load and probably start looking for jobs elsewhere or worse, give customers misleading information.

By explaining things and sharing your targets and business strategy with them they'll feel part of the change management process. This will motivate them and encourage them to share the burden with you.

It's also only human to struggle with change. In many cases, EMU is going to challenge your working environment and this will upset the equilibrium among any staff, who may find themselves having to do things differently. This will make them feel vulnerable and exposed, particularly if it requires changing a life-long set of habits and systems. No doubt you'll be feeling a bit vulnerable too, so communicate with your staff and work together as a team: that way you'll get much better results.

Remember, your staff are your best ambassadors: if they feel confident and happy in their working environment they'll tell other people about your firm and speak highly of it. If negative rumours start to circulate, you can, with good communications, stamp them out quickly and put the record straight so they don't gain momentum by default.

You can also use some of the messages you are putting across in your internal communications programme for an external programme. Your customers, suppliers, etc also need to know what you're doing and why.

What Can a Good Communications Programme Achieve?

It can improve your bottom line:

▌ by promoting your business vision and values

▌ it will inspire and guide those to whom you are trying to communicate

▌ it will soften the blow of bad or unwelcome news, eg redundancies

▌ it'll unite your workforce towards achieving corporate goals

▌ it should help you to sell your products/services

▌ it should help you to accelerate the speed at which your business develops.

As mentioned earlier, a good communications programme will stop negative messages gaining momentum by default. You will be in control of the messages that are put out before the rumour mill starts running. This will also help you during difficult times.

Finally, a good internal communications programme will:

▌ help your staff adapt to change

▌ let your staff know that you care and are willing to take the time to communicate with them

▌ raise awareness among your workforce about the issues you are facing and what issues they should give priority to themselves

▌ motivate your workforce. Informed staff who know exactly where the company is going and what it is trying to achieve will be more inclined to get on with their work rather than stand around bitching about everything they don't like. If you have a good feedback system, they'll also feel that senior management is listening to them. This will go a long way to making them feel better about the changes taking place around them, particularly if you are in a position to put right some of the things they don't like.

What are the key points to consider in an internal communications programme?

▮ Ensure that all your communication efforts are targeted towards your long-term business objectives.

▮ Create a list of the people to whom you need to communicate.

▮ Tailor your message to each specific audience. This is an art in itself but there is a useful rule of thumb: put yourself in the shoes of the recipient. Imagine how you would respond to the message that's being conveyed if you were on the receiving end. All too frequently senior management communicate with only themselves in mind rather than their staff. The result is that your employees receive information that turns them off and defeats the whole purpose of trying to communicate in the first place. The only place for filing such information is in the bin.

▮ Manage your programme, so the flow of information remains consistent and constant. There's no point embarking on an all-singing, all-dancing programme that is abandoned in two months' time. If you're going to launch a staff newsletter, for example, you have to make sure that you publish it regularly.

What Tools and Systems Can I Use to Enhance Communications Within my Organization?

Once you've assessed what your business needs to do to take advantage of the new business climate EMU will create, review your existing communications strategy and what you've been doing to date.

What Sort of Tools Can I Use to Communicate These Important Changes to my Employees?

Each company has different requirements but there are basic methods you can think about:

- line managers
- internet/intranet
- staff newsletter/brochure
- video/CD-ROM
- video and telephone conferences
- seminars/workshops.

Line managers

The best way to communicate is face-to-face, so make sure you cascade the most important messages down to your staff either by hosting staff meetings yourself or via your line managers. This allows your employees the opportunity for interactive discussion. It's obviously better to host these sessions with small groups rather than with large numbers – people feel intimidated when asking questions in front of large audiences.

Internet/intranet

If you already have a company website, consider setting up an EMU website which can be accessed by your employees and maybe your customers if you want.

Check out other company websites for ideas on how to set this up, and use it as a tool to communicate your business strategy, new internal developments within your company, news on EMU, etc.

Newsletter

Create an EMU newsletter for distribution to your staff giving them up-dates on your progress towards meeting the challenges of EMU.

Brochure

Publish a brochure or booklet that provides a guide to EMU.

Seminars and workshops

Host staff seminars and workshops to provide a platform for interactive discussion on EMU.

Videos/CD-ROM

If you have the budget, you could use video and/or CD-ROM. These can be adapted and modified for other uses too.

For example a video which has a standard presentation about the corporate vision of your company could be adapted for use by your sales force and tailored to specific products, or for a specific presentation. It can also be used for training, for recruitment, etc.

Video/telephone conferences

If you have employees in different locations and it's difficult to communicate the important messages to everyone at once, arrange to do so either by telephone conference calls or via video conferencing. This enables you to speak to everyone at once and ensures that the really important messages don't get misinterpreted as they feed through the system – you don't want Chinese Whispers to lead to distorted messages being communicated.

What Sort of Things Should I be Considering When it Comes to Communicating With my Staff?

Think of your staff as individuals who are going to be affected by EMU both in and out of work. They're consumers, savers, ordinary citizens, future pensioners and borrowers, as well as your employees. So when thinking about issues that they need to address, think about how EMU will affect them on these fronts as well as at work.

Consider putting together an information pack about all these issues, including an explanation of how, if at all, your own staff pension scheme, benefits systems, etc may change as a result of EMU, as well as some general background about what they should expect to see. Some examples of what to put in would be some of the basic facts about the euro, such as the following.

What does economic and monetary union mean?

Economic and Monetary Union (EMU) will involve the creation of a single monetary policy within Europe. This policy, which will set interest and exchange rates, will only apply to those countries which join EMU. However, there is also something called the growth and stability pact which requires countries which are in EMU or are thinking of joining it to meet certain economic criteria. If Britain wants to keep its options open to be able to join EMU in the future, the Government will try to stay in line with the monetary policies that have been laid out by Europe.

Why did the European Union decide to introduce a single currency?

For more than three decades now, the European vision has included an agenda for creating a single currency. Latterly it was seen as the only way to put the finishing touches to the creation of a Single Market within Europe.

You could argue that we already have a Single Market, so why do we need a single currency too?

While we do in theory have a Single Market, we're still exposed to exchange rate fluctuations which create additional costs and inefficiencies for companies trading within Europe. The euro is designed to stop this.

When will I actually be able to put euro notes and coins in my pocket?

At the latest, on 1 January 2002. By 1 July 2002, all member countries will have their own national currencies withdrawn from circulation, so if you go to France or Holland, for instance, you'll find that your francs or guilders won't be legal tender anymore. However, if you find yourself stuck with a wad of French francs, you'll still be able to exchange them for euros free of charge in France.

If there's going to be one monetary policy for all, will that affect my tax bill?

No, the British Government will still be in control of our tax bills.

What will the euro look like? Will it be the same in all Member States?

Yes, the euro will look the same, but on the notes there'll be a small space on one side to allow the issuing country to be identified. So, for example, if Britain joins, we should be able to put a picture of the Queen on one side of our euros.

What denominations will the euro be issued in?

Notes will be printed in denominations of 5, 10, 20, 50, 100, 200 and 500 euros. And there will be eight new coins. The euro itself will be divided up into 100 cents, like the pound into 100 pence. The coins will range from one-hundredth of a euro (like the penny) to 1 euro, and there will also be a coin that's worth 2 euros.

What will happen on 1 January 1999?

This is the date when Europe physically starts the process of introducing the euro into the market place. The conversion rates of participating countries will be fixed, eg the value of the DM to the euro will be irrevocably set, the governments of member countries will switch their national bonds to euros, and the national banks of these countries will start to adopt the new policies set out by the European Central Bank. This means that the individual central banks, through something called the European System of Central Banks (ESCB), will also conduct all their monetary and foreign-exchange operations in euros.

And finally, a lot of companies, institutional investors, banks, etc will start using euros instead of national currencies for non-paper financial transactions.

How will this new monetary policy affect my mortgage if the ECB is going to be setting interest rates from 1 January 1999?

In order to prepare for our possible entry into EMU, the Bank of England is likely to try and match the interest rates set in Europe. As they're considerably lower than ours, it means interest rates will in the longer term come down. But that's going to be dependent on whether or not inflation starts creeping up. If it does, the Bank of England will be reluctant to lower interest rates and, if they do, it'll be a gradual process.

If Britain decides it's going to join EMU, it may be worth looking at taking out new mortgages with long-term fixed rates, alternatively switching an existing variable rate mortgage to one with a fixed term. You'll need to seek independent advice on this issue before making up your mind, and don't think about it until Britain has made a final decision, otherwise you may end up paying more because interest rates are closely linked to inflation.

What is the European Commission?

The equivalent of our civil service, it is responsible for proposing legislation, mediating between governments to try and get their agreement on future legislation, managing the technical details of policy, representing the EC at international conferences and summits, defending the collective interests of the EC and making sure that EC law is upheld. In total it employs around 20,000 people.

What is the European Council?

This is probably the most powerful body within the EU. It's made up of the heads of each Member State's government (in our case Tony Blair), and foreign ministers, a Commission president and a vice-president. The members of the council meet every six months to discuss the future strategic development of the EU.

Is Training Going to be Important?

Yes, it's going to be essential, but you don't have to do it all in one go. By prioritizing you can do it in stages and keep the costs down.

Ask your EMU manager to assess which staff should get precedence. A rough guideline would be to give priority to those who will actually be managing the changes within your business (eg, those people who work in accounting, finance and information systems).

You should also give specific attention to people who have direct contact with your clients. They're bound to be asked questions about the impact of EMU on your business and how it might affect their trading relationship with you, so these staff need to be armed with all the right answers.

People in sales and procurement will also need to understand how the euro works, especially if you're going to expect them to be able to negotiate within the dual currency system on your behalf. During the three year transition period from 1 January 1999 to 2002, they'll have to contend with trading in the euro and/or possibly the national currencies of participating EMU members too. In order to get the best deals, they're going to have to fully understand what's at stake and how it all works.

What Do I Do About Wage and Pension Conversion if Britain Joins EMU, or Within my European Subsidiary Offices?

The conversion timetable for pay-slips into euros will vary according to each individual member country but the deadline for 'in' countries is 1 January 2002. For the UK, it will probably not be an issue until 2005.

This will mean that personnel managers will have to be able to explain the lay-out of the new pay-slips and give details of how the old salary has been converted into euros. This is particularly important if someone's pay is affected by rounding differences. This process is likely to be unwieldy and time-consuming so allow plenty of preparation for it.

Before you switch over to paying your staff in euros you'll have to explain to them what is involved, when you'll do it and why you're doing it. You may also need to set up some sort of advice service so they can ask questions and feel more comfortable about the whole process.

If you want to phase in the conversion to paying your staff in euros, for a time you could present the amount you've paid on pay-slips in both currencies. It'll be up to you to decide when to start and how long you're going to keep it up.

I Have Employees in Some of the Euro-zone Countries. What Issues Should I be Considering For Them?

▌ You'll have to start by reviewing their contracts. You may at the same time have to look at the contracts of your employees working in non EMU member countries such as Britain because once everything is expressed in euros, it'll be easier for comparisons to be made between staff. You'll have to watch out: it could be the start of wage increases creeping in. You'll also need to anticipate the impact of rounding on salaries and how this might affect your budgets. There may also be charges associated with the administrative costs of converting the salaries of your European employees, so you'll have to provide for that.

If I'm Going to Convert to Paying my Staff in Euros, What do I do About Commissions and Bonuses?

Unless you wish to change the time at which you have traditionally paid your staff the variable part of their salary, you could take a similar approach to the one you do with salary conversion. If you want to use EMU as an opportunity to change the timing of bonus and commission payments, you'll need to explain the rationale for this and the convergence criteria to your employees.

How About the Need for Liaison With Union Representatives?

Needless to say, pay is usually a sensitive area, so if you're in any doubt about the implications of converting people's pay, pension, etc into euros, it may be a good idea to do it in consultation with their union or works council representative. If you do ask your staff if they would like to be paid in euros rather than Sterling be careful not to let them think you are doing this in order to pass on your currency risk to your employees.

Critics of EMU Say the Labour Markets Will Have to be Reformed Before it Can Work. Is the Burden of Reform Likely to Trickle Down to Companies Themselves?

Yes, companies will have a role to play if a serious effort is going to be made to bring down unemployment figures. But that doesn't mean that you'll be forced to hire people you don't want.

The reality is that government initiatives alone won't succeed in improving training and skills to create a more flexible workforce; some of the onus is going to fall on individual businesses.

We all know that we can no longer expect a job for life, but to ensure that you attract the best employees, you might need to make changes to your own working practices. Highly skilled people come at a premium, so it might be in your own interests to create skilled people and keep them happy so they stay with your company. This may require a radical re-think on how you treat and train them.

There Has Been Talk About Product-market Reform. Will This Affect Employment Issues?

Yes, because if you can create a company that is dynamic and flexible, producing new products, new services, etc as the markets change, you'll create new employment opportunities as well as increasing your own company's profits.

15 *Marketing and Trade*

If Competition is Going to Heat Up, How Can I Win the Trade War?

Many SMEs feel that the introduction of the euro means that they will simply have to ensure they can invoice in euros. But it is also about ensuring you still have customers to invoice.

Nearly one-third of the world's trade is denominated in euro-zone currencies. With its planned expansion to 15 members by 2002, the EMU region will become the world's largest economic block with 30 per cent of world trade – almost double the current amount.

How Will the Euro Impact on my Trade?

Economists predict that the euro will force companies to slash prices, trim suppliers and streamline production. This is because the common currency will highlight pricing disparities, and ease of conversion from one currency to another – without exchange costs or risks – will make it far easier for companies to shop around.

Businesses that compete well will be able to grab market share. However, this could also mean that profit margins will be squeezed and corporations will have to be leaner.

How Will it Impact on Those I Trade With?

With currency risks gone, companies can expand and start to look at cross-border trading – that means that companies from Europe will start to look at trading their wares in the UK too. EMU Member States – generally to the south and east of Europe – with lower taxes, wages and other overheads, will become more appealing. Therefore, you could find that while you have adapted your business to become more competitive, you have lost the companies you do business with to another European country.

How Can my Company Look to Compete if European Companies Start to Flood Britain With Products Like Mine?

Retaliate – when you looked at how your business will be affected by EMU you probably spotted opportunities for you to explore; follow these through. If you don't have the resources to physically send out sales and new business development people to explore and develop new business opportunities, consider using the internet as a means of selling.

Paul Taffe, Managing Director of Hill & Knowlton, the international communications consultancy, says dual pricing is already coming in and companies in the UK, particularly those in the business-to-business market, will have no choice but to fall into line with what becomes common business practice. Therefore there's no chance now of using dual pricing as a marketing initiative; the opportunity has been and gone. British companies are part of the supply chain and they're just having to follow the crowd.

He says one of the most powerful tools at the disposal of companies who don't have huge business development capital at their disposal is the internet. Although the use of the internet is catching on fast in Britain, we still lag behind some other countries – for example in Finland, where there's a population of about 1.5 million people, approximately 60,000 of them are plugged into the internet.

As more and more people and businesses start using the internet to shop and to find out about products, services and other things that interest them, you too will have an opportunity to sell your products and services. The internet is a global system so you could find yourself selling your products far more widely than just in Europe.

Hill & Knowlton's Paul Taffe says that the key to creating a good website is to make sure you do it in several languages. For example if you want to start expanding into Germany, create a website in German as well as English. 'The internet is driving cost-efficient sales for many companies.' He adds: 'The internet is a very retail-based system and it's something that's a little bit different.'

Before you start thinking of using the internet as a means of expanding your business, consider what the cost of transporting your goods/services is going to be – if you can send items cheaply or visit these countries to service the orders, that's great; if not, perhaps you'd better reconsider your plans.

Finally, it's very important that your website responds to simple search requests. Most people source internet information by 'surfing' the web, so you have to have pertinent links to the web's search engines. There are a number of companies which can advise you on how to set up a website; alternatively, if you're feeling brave you can do it yourself.

Should I Consider Embarking on a Proactive Marketing Programme if I Want to Expand?

Yes, particularly if you want to reach new customers.

What Can a Good Communications Programme Achieve?

It can improve your bottom line:

▮ by helping you to accelerate the speed at which your business develops

▮ it should also help you to generate third-party endorsement of your business and products via the press and people/staff talking favourably about the company, particularly if you embark on a press relations campaign

▮ advertising and marketing will also help to create brand awareness for your business and your products.

What are the Key Points to Consider in an External Communications Programme?

▌ Ensure that all your communication efforts are targeted towards your long-term business objectives.

▌ Create a list of the people to whom you need to communicate, eg staff, investors, customers, suppliers, unions, regulatory bodies, trade associations, the media.

▌ Tailor your message to each specific audience. As we said in the previous chapter, this is an art in itself, but stick to the basis of putting yourself in the shoes of the recipient and imagine how you would respond to the message that's being conveyed if you were on the receiving end.

▌ Manage your programme so that the flow of information remains consistent and constant. There's no point embarking on an all-singing, all-dancing programme that you drop in two months' time. If you're going to advertise, one advert appearing once is unlikely to produce any long-term benefits.

What Tools and Systems Can I Use to Promote my Business?

Once you've assessed what your business needs to do to take advantage of the new business climate EMU will create, review your existing communications strategy or what you've been doing to date to promote and market your business. Now think about the vehicles you can use to communicate your corporate and product messages.

Speaking at conferences

This can be a very good way to broaden your reach. But before accepting or offering to speak at a conference find out who the delegates are going to be: there is little point in you spending a great deal of time preparing a presentation on your industry's trends if all you're going to be doing is talking to your competition.

Hosting seminars

If you have something new and exciting to talk about – such as a new invention or a business development – there may be an opportunity for you to host a seminar for your clients.

For example, a lot of banks are hosting seminars and workshops on EMU for their clients to ensure that they are ready for EMU too. This is particularly important for the big investment banks who need to make sure their clients understand what's involved with EMU and are well prepared for it. If these clients start dithering and don't know which currency they're going to use it'll cause delays and serious gridlock in the banks' support systems, creating cancelled orders, etc. This would cause mayhem and the banks are keen to avoid this. But EMU also provides the banks with an opportunity to touch base with their customers – it also gives them a means of promoting their services. You could look at doing something similar – although EMU may not be the right topic for your business, there will be other opportunities for you to identify.

Alternatively, if you can't find a subject that you think would be of interest to your customers, maybe one of your customers or suppliers is planning to host a seminar on a subject for clients in which you could participate.

Marketing literature

If you're going to switch to a dual pricing environment you'll have to reprint all your sales and marketing literature. If this is the case think about the opportunity of printing a new corporate brochure which outlines your views of the future and your business objectives, and tells prospective clients about your products and services and how they can help. Perhaps you could include a case study of one or two of your clients who may be willing to endorse your business, details about the management structure, etc.

Internet

See earlier in this chapter.

Corporate videos and CD-ROMs

In addition to helping you with your internal communication and training requirements, videos and CD-ROMs can also be very helpful when you want to show people what your company does and how it does it.

If you want to use a video for a number of audiences but maintain the same theme throughout, you don't necessarily have to make different recordings. For example if you're already planning to commission a company to make you a video for training purposes, ask them to shoot extra footage of your factory floor/company and its surroundings, maybe even some extra interviews with your senior management and staff as well – the questions may vary slightly depending on how you want to use the video. From this core footage, you can then make several different videos at the same time; you'll just need to change the script, some of the interview sequences and footage. All this can be done in the editing room and it'll save you a lot of money.

You can then use the footage to create CD-ROMs which can be incorporated into formal presentations made on your computer, eg power point presentations. These can be up-dated and modified very easily. They also provide you with a very impressive set of presentation tools which should prove to be invaluable.

Merchandising

The merchandising business is vast and growing all the time, from Cindy doll lunch boxes to monogrammed clocks from Tiffany: you name the product and it can be done.

If you want to look at ways of promoting your business and trademark through consumer items which you either give away as corporate gifts or sell, it's a good way of getting your name out – but think about it before you go off spending a fortune on thousands of T-shirts.

You need to consider who you're going to give or sell the products to, which product appropriately reflects your image, and why anybody would want what you have to offer. One company I worked with in the past had some beautiful Tiffany pocket-size atlases. We did not in fact have them inscribed with anything because it was felt this would cheapen the product – the strategy was to give people a beautiful gift which would be useful. By using the gift, it was hoped that the recipients of the gift would by association remember the company. So, you don't always have to ram the message down people's throats to make the association with your company.

Sponsorship

Sponsoring an event, art exhibition, football team, whatever, can be a very useful way of promoting your company – sponsorship, like advertising, can cost millions and millions or it can be for very small amounts. No doubt you already receive requests from local sports teams, schools, arts organizations, etc asking you to give financial support to something or other. There can be a multitude of reasons for saying yes or no to a sponsorship deal; here are some guidelines.

1. Think about how sponsoring a particular thing will benefit your business. Will it generate goodwill from someone or in an area that is important to your business?
2. Can you use it as an opportunity to invite clients, suppliers, etc along, as a means of getting to know them better?
3. Will it help you to recruit new staff? Say you need school-leavers; you could consider sponsoring a local school football team.
4. Can you generate publicity out of your sponsorship?
5. Are you doing it because it's a whim, or you personally like the idea, or does it fit in with your corporate objectives? Sponsorship has to reflect your key corporate messages and reflect your business image. An extreme example would be the British Race Horse Society sponsoring the Crufts dog show – they don't quite fit do they?
6. If you do decide to sponsor an event you should find out how many other sponsors will be involved and what type of accreditation your company will receive and where – you must be happy with the profile you're going to receive, otherwise don't do it.
7. In the accreditation you receive as a sponsor you'll probably have an opportunity to write a short description of your business, so if you want to reflect the fact that your business is very creative and innovative you could think about sponsoring a

theatre group which has the same corporate identity as you. If you want to reflect the fact that you're strong and stable, perhaps you should go for an 'old masters' art exhibition.

Community affairs

A good community affairs programme will show your commitment as a good, responsible corporate citizen; there can also be tax advantages if you link it up with making charitable donations. Again though, you should focus on which charities and projects you commit your support to; in many cases it's better not to spread yourself too thinly. By giving time as well as money to fewer initiatives you'll be able to make a bigger contribution and ultimately help more; you'll also get greater recognition for what you do.

Advertising

Advertising can be rather expensive and it only works if you have a clear idea of what you want to get out of it and why you're doing it. If you plan to embark on a major international advertising campaign it can cost millions, but if you want to keep it low key and cheap this is also attainable. However, sometimes direct marketing or a public relations campaign can be more beneficial and cost-efficient. Take advice before you make a decision.

Direct marketing

This may involve mail shots to current and potential customers. If you need names and addresses you can buy mailing lists; for example some magazines will rent out their subscription mailing lists. So if you were wanting to sell do-it-yourself car maintenance kits you could perhaps rent the subscription list from one of the car magazines; the same sort of thing would apply to golf balls and a golfing magazine. If you are offering business services, you could try one of the business magazines, and so on.

The press

If you don't already do it, think about embarking on a public relations programme so that journalists write about your company and your products. You may need to consider hiring a PR agency to help you with this or hiring a specialist to work in-house, because it's not as easy as it appears. Everything you say and do will have repercussions on your business because articles that appear in the press about you can affect your sales, your staff, your share price, etc. The advantage of seeing your company written up in newspapers and magazines is that it gives you and your products third-party endorsement which in turn gives credibility to what you're saying. The value of good press coverage is immeasurable and can make a big difference to your business.

But beware, journalists will look objectively at what you're telling them, so never tell them lies and be prepared to take criticism as well as applause. You have no control over what they write or broadcast unless you are paying for the coverage in the form of an 'advertorial'. This means that you buy the space in which the article is going to appear rather like an advertisement; it does not give you the same credibility as an independent article but it does give you more control and it provides you with an opportunity to communicate your message.

If I Want to Embark on a PR Campaign What do I Need to Do to Prepare For It?

Sir John Harvey-Jones, former chairman of ICI, once said:

> Most of our time in business is spent in communication – either in listening, or in trying to persuade others . . . Even more to the point, when you present your case badly or ambiguously, you not only let yourself down but also all the people who work for your organization. You are their representative, in many cases the only person who can speak for them and they deserve the best that you can do.

So time spent preparing for a press interview is never wasted. Before you even agree to an interview, you must know why you're doing it and what you want to achieve from it. Sometimes it may be better to politely decline.

An entire book could be written – and a number have been written – purely on the subject of public relations and it may be worth your while taking some time out to have some training on interview technique before you start doing interviews. A number of practising and former journalists are setting up companies precisely to give people media training. It costs on average about £1,800 for a full day, which includes training for TV, radio and print interviews. Here are a few tips.

1.   Avoid using jargon or colloquial English.
2.   Never assume that what you say is off the record – only go 'off the record', which means the journalist won't use what you say, if you know and trust the journalist to whom you are speaking. It's very easy for a journalist to flick through their notes and to inadvertently use something you did not want them to. If you need to give some background information to put something into context then do so, but be prepared to see it repeated.
3.   Speak slowly and clearly and if you're talking about something complex ask the journalist if they've understood what you've said.
4.   If you're doing an interview for broadcasting, use short sentences and keep your answers concise and clear.
5.   If you don't understand the question or feel uncomfortable with it, ask the journalist to repeat it.
6.   If you're caught unawares by a journalist who calls you and asks you about something awkward, buy time and say you'll call them back within an agreed time frame to give you time to prepare before you answer their questions.
7.   Always be sensitive to the pressures a journalist is under: they have deadlines and pressure too, so ask them what their deadline is and always call them when you say you will. If you can't call them, forewarn them. If you're trying to raise your press profile and you don't return their calls they'll soon go to another company who does and that could be one of your competitors!
8.   If more than one person in your organization is speaking to the press make sure they all know your company policy with regard to press relations and that everyone is singing from the same hymn sheet.

9. Finally, monitor your press coverage. You need to know what the general feelings are towards your company – you can put things right if they're going wrong or continue with what you're doing if it's working.

What Are Some of the Key Issues I Need to Consider to Communicate Effectively?

You want your audiences to hear, read and see what you have to say, otherwise you're not communicating. So communicate in the language your audience will understand and relate to. If you're having difficulties in getting the message across it's you who has the problem, not your audience.

Know what your audience is looking to hear, read and see before you start; that way you can tailor your messages to meet their own expectations. If you don't they'll resist your communications efforts.

Make sure all your communication efforts support your business goals and strategy and always have those in the back of your mind before you do anything.

If Legislation is Going to be Passed That Could Harm my Business Can I do Anything to Try and Stop It?

Yes, you can – either contact your trade association and ask them to represent you in a lobbying campaign as part of an industry-wide initiative or hire a lobbyist on your behalf.

What Sales Opportunities Does the Euro Present?

If you went to some shops in northern France in early 1998 you would have found some goods priced in euros – even though euros did not exist! These retailers obviously see the euro as more than a marketing gimmick. For a start, the idea of the single currency tends to appeal to younger, better educated and therefore more affluent Europeans.

How Can I Ensure my Products Will Sell Well Abroad?

The most important factor after price is that they meet European Standards. These relate to packaging, weights and measures, sizes and warning labels.

How Can I Get Help to Export?

You local Business Link will probably have an international trade team. This will have access to the Department of Trade and Industry, The Foreign Office, Chambers of Commerce plus Export Development Counsellors and experts from Overseas Trade Services. Every export support body is now linked to a single source which can give you world market and product information. The telephone number is 07000 40 50 60.

16 EMU Checklist

This chapter is set out in two sections. The first deals with the areas of your business you need to look at. The second contains brainstorming prompts – questions you should at least ask even if you feel you do not need to act upon any changes immediately.

Areas to Look At

Set up a taskforce

The taskforce needn't be large; it could be just one or two people.

▪ Does your business have a strategy to deal with EMU?

▪ Is your strategy flexible enough to take into account the changing UK position and development of EMU?

When Siemens created its euro taskforce in 1995, it was solely made up of finance people, but the company realized very soon that it was not a pure finance issue. Remember to include your finance, human resources and information technology departments/personnel on the team.

Assess the impact of EMU on your business

When will you be asked to adopt the euro? Talk to:

▪ customers

▪ suppliers.

Look at how this will affect different aspects of your business

▌ Information technology/systems.

▌ Accounting.

▌ Pricing of products.

▌ Sales.

▌ Marketing and reprinting of sales literature.

▌ Staff training.

▌ Competition.

Devise a plan to prepare your business

Talk to:

▌ your bank

▌ software suppliers

▌ outside consultants (lawyer/accountant)

▌ competitors.

Allocate responsibility for managing the changeover. Set your company a timetable to compete your EMU preparations.

Inform others of your decision

Let people know when, if and how you will work with the euro and what your plans are. Tell:

▌ customers

▌ suppliers

▌ shareholders/investors

▌ staff.

Brainstorming Questions

Managing the changeover

1. What lead times are required to implement the necessary changes to the organization?
2. What internal/external resources will be needed?
3. What information do I need to ensure a successful transition?
4. How will the changeover be coordinated throughout the company?

Products

1. Is there an opportunity to develop new products and services?
2. Will my existing range of products and services need to be adjusted as a result of the single currency?

Pricing in euros

1. When is the euro likely to be used as an invoicing currency in my market(s)?
2. Are there large price differences between my products and services and those on offer from my European competitors?
3. How should I react to large price differences, if at all?
4. How should I deal with tax discrepancies on my products in different countries? Should I set prices that make all of them identical at pre-tax prices throughout Europe?
5. Will the price of my products need adjusting, particularly low-value items, above and beyond the straight conversion rates from Sterling into euros to make them more competitive?
6. If I have to re-price my products how can I ensure I don't lose out financially?

Suppliers

1. Will foreign suppliers start competing for business in my market – should I too start looking for non-UK suppliers?
2. Will the euro create greater competition among my suppliers and start a price war?

3. Will the euro open up an opportunity to review current pricing agreements with suppliers or to review existing contracts?
4. Should I ask non EMU-zone suppliers to price their invoices in euros? If so, when?
5. Have all these issues been discussed with the procurement team?
6. When, if at all, will my own suppliers start using euros?

Payment conditions

1. Will the terms for payment to my suppliers and customers need to be altered to unify them?
2. Will the euro create an opportunity for me to improve current payment conditions and reduce bank finance?

Impact on electronic ordering

1. How will I convert my electronic ordering and order processing systems so that they can handle euro transactions?
2. Will I have to operate in a multi-currency environment during the EMU transition period?
3. Have all the necessary regulatory procedures been dealt with to use Electronic Data Interchange (EDI) – if not how much time is needed to make the necessary preparations?

Procurement and logistics

1. Will I be able to find cheaper non-UK suppliers?
2. Should I review supplier prices and look for non-UK suppliers?
3. With all the changes that are taking place in my marketing and procurement strategies, do I need to adjust our logistical activities such as the services we use for delivering and receiving goods if for example we change our payment conditions?
4. Will I need to increase/decrease our storage facilities to account for a change in payment conditions, business expansion, etc?
5. During the transition period how will I treat the euro – as another currency or as a reference currency for pooling/netting?

Treasury and banking services

1. Which services do we currently use for pooling, netting or automatic exchange of balances? Will these services be affected by the euro?
2. Will the single currency create opportunities to modify our existing systems for paying an invoice/charging in a foreign currency or receiving payments?
3. How much of our hedging operations will still be necessary after 1999?
4. How will we cope with currency risk in the future if we've never had to do so in the past (eg, if you receive EU grants in ECU)?

Impact on financing

1. Will the capital markets offer me new opportunities to raise funds and if so how will the euro affect my decision?
2. Should I use the capital markets for bonds, equity, loans?

Bank relationships

1. Can I reduce the number of bank accounts I currently use?
2. Will the introduction of a single currency give me an opportunity to reduce my banking charges?
3. What euro-related services do I need from my bank(s)?
4. Do I need to speak to my bank about the euro and what it's offering to its clients in the form of advice, new products and services, etc?
5. Will my bank charge me to convert to using euros and, if so, how much?

Marketing

1. Will the euro create opportunities to develop our European exports? If so, for which products and in which markets?
2. Will we be able to target new customer groups?
3. Should we plan to launch a new marketing effort in their direction?
4. How will the euro impact on our customers – will they start looking to buy from our European competitors?

5. Will the markets of my major customers change as a result of the euro and how is that likely to affect my business?
6. Are our key competitors operating in just the UK or in other countries too?
7. Will EMU change the competitive environment and if so how?
8. Will my market be exposed to increased competition and how should I react to this?

Sales

1. What impact will the single currency have on my commercial activities?
2. As a result of the single currency and reduced currency risk exposure should I now consider my European sales efforts as domestic or foreign?
3. Can I use the euro as an opportunity to review the way the company's markets are currently segmented?
4. Should I reorganize my sales force?
5. Does the euro create opportunities to try new sales techniques, such as using the internet, direct marketing, etc?
6. Are there any opportunities to strike new strategic alliances with distributors, competitors, suppliers, etc?

External communication

1. Have we identified all the documentation that needs to be reprinted, prepared to cope with new pricing structures, products, etc?
2. How shall I tell my customers about the company's decision to switch to using euros or both Sterling and euros?
3. Can I use EMU as a marketing tool?
4. Do I need to contact my long-term customers to review the consequences of the euro on their own businesses?
5. Do I need to offer my customers advice and information about the euro?
6. What training schemes do I need to introduce for my staff who interact with customers?
7. Should I get in touch with my trade association to make sure I have the most up-to-date information available?

Using the euro during the transition period (1999–2002)

1. When should I start invoicing in euros? What factors will influence this decision (international sales, customer demand, competitors doing so, public procurement contracts, etc)?
2. Will some of my major customers switch to using the euro and, if so, would they prefer it if I did too?
3. If I need to start invoicing in both euros and Sterling how should I do it?
4. What costs are going to be involved in preparing for the euro?
5. Do I need to set up Electronic Data Interchange (EDI) links with my customers? If so, will they be converting to using euros too?
6. Are my sales administration systems capable of working in both denominations or will I have to modify them?

Pension provision

1. Should I change the way the company pension and my own pension, company investments, etc are managed, to take advantage of the changing investment climate in Europe?

Shares

1. From 4 January next year, most of Europe's stock exchanges have said they'll quote share prices in euros – should I consider re-denominating my shares into euros? (If your company is already listed on one of the new euro stock markets, you'll have to provide financial information in euros. Do you have historical data that can be re-priced in euros?)
2. If I need to re-denominate my shares into euros, I'll have to modify the statutes of my company. Am I prepared for this scenario?

Human resources

1. How and when will I convert wages and pensions into euros?
2. How will I communicate these changes to my employees?
3. Should I start by presenting employees' pay in both currencies for a while? If so, when should I do so and for how long?

4. How will I inform the unions/work councils of my plans? Should I involve them in the decision making process?
5. How will I motivate my employees and encourage them to take an active role in the changeover process?
6. How will I decide which areas of my business need to be able to deal with euros first?
7. How will I initiate training on the euro for my staff and in what order?
8. How will the changeover process be coordinated within my firm?

Accounting and taxation

1. Will I need to operate in a dual currency environment with the euro as well as other currencies? If so, when, for how long and in which currencies?
2. When will I convert my accounts to the euro?
3. When should I publish our annual report and consolidated accounts in euros and do they need to be authorized by a British auditor?
4. Will the euro increase the risk of error – if so, what safeguards can I introduce?
5. How will I account for the costs of conversion – write them off through the profit and loss account or create provisions, etc?
6. How will I treat rounding differences resulting from conversions between the euro and national currencies?
7. Should I consider subcontracting some or all of my accounting requirements to deal with the transition period?
8. Should I plan for the conversion of our equity? Should I round the nominal value of shares in euros and will this require an extraordinary general meeting?
9. When will I convert our dividends to euros and how will I inform the shareholders?
10. Will the company statutes need to be adjusted? Should I take legal advice?

Taxation

1. Will my company have assets and liabilities in the currencies of participating EMU countries at the end of this year? If so,

will they be liable to tax if gains or losses are made once the conversion rates have been fixed on 31 December 1998?

2. Will I have an opportunity to make our tax declarations and other statutory returns (eg company accounts) in euros during the transitional period and if so would it be useful to do so?

3. How will rounding differences on capital be treated from a fiscal point of view?

4. How should I manage tax discrepancies on our products in the EU and will we apply identical pre-tax prices throughout Europe?

Information systems

1. What information systems do we currently use, which ones will need up-dates or replacement, and can we deal with the Year 2000 problems at the same time?

2. Have we started preparing for the Year 2000 issue? If so, can we link up these preparations to the euro preparations?

3. Is there going to be an opportunity to replace our existing software with a standard package compatible with the euro?

4. Have I allowed time and money to train staff for the new software we will install?

5. Will we be able to easily identify the aspects of our IT facilities that will need adapting?

6. Have I allowed time to evaluate existing systems and do test runs on new systems before we go live?

7. Will we be able to make our systems more customer-oriented to improve our data bases during our preparations?

Company Reports

British Steel

British Steel began to prepare for the introduction of the single currency in 1996 in tandem with its preparations for the Millennium.

In 1996, the company set up an informal group. This group was given the task of identifying the issues that needed to be addressed and working out how the preparations should be conducted.

In 1997, a unit dedicated to EMU was set up. The main areas that it needed to address were its commercial, financial and logistical operations. At this time it was decided that the best way to implement the changes would be to make each individual business within British Steel – 14 in all – responsible for its own preparations. Each unit then reports to the head office task force which in turn reports to a central steering group.

A spokesman for the company says it is going to cost about £2 million to make all the necessary preparations, but it was too early to say whether or not in the long term it would actually save the company money because initially it makes things more complex.

Approximately one-third of British Steel's products are sold in continental Europe, one-half in the UK and the remaining 20 per cent in the rest of the world. In the long term, that means that 80 per cent of its business could be conducted in one currency if Britain joins EMU; if it doesn't it'll be just one-third. Even so, the cost savings on cross-border currency transactions should be significant.

In a recent statement to the press, British Steel said it had no immediate plans to impose a change to current commercial arrangements with its suppliers. In common with many other companies, it is now preparing its financial and commercial systems so that it can pay and receive in euros. However, the company is keen to emphasize that it has no plans to force its suppliers to switch to receiving payment in euros.

British Steel wants Britain to join EMU and is encouraging the government to work with its EU partners to create the right conditions for a sustainable single currency. When the economic conditions are right the company says we should join the single currency. At the moment, it says the pound is 'clearly uncompetitive and while it remains above 2.50 deutschmarks to the pound, it is a big problem for British manufacturers'.

The company's spokesman said: 'In theory any supplier who wishes to be paid in euros will be able to do so, which will of course reduce our exposure to European currencies. We'll also be able to receive payment in euros.'

Currently, the company buys about 20 million tonnes of iron ore from countries such as Brazil and Australia, and 20 million tonnes of coal from the USA, Canada, Australia and Germany. The internationally accepted currency for these deals is the US dollar. In the short term British Steel doesn't see this changing, but in the longer term, if the euro works, these deals may start to be done in euros. If this happens, says British Steel, it would make life a lot easier.

While it's early days, and too soon for the company to say whether or not it's going to switch totally to the euro as its main trading currency, the company is already taking advantage of the new opportunities emerging to raise money (as outlined in Chapter 9, Borrowing, grants and raising finance). It recently issued a £200 million, ten-year Sterling bond. This is the first time British Steel has sought to raise money from the bond markets; it previously financed expansion plans from existing revenues.

Marks & Spencer

The retail chain Marks & Spencer has outlets in Ireland, France, Germany, Spain, Holland and Belgium as well as in other non Euro-zone countries, including of course the UK.

It was one of the first companies to announce that whether Britain is in or out of EMU, it's going to be ready to trade in parallel currencies. This means that it will be in a position to trade in both euros and the national currency of the country in which it is operating.

It also warns that this is going to be a testing time because customers are going to feel threatened and confused by the change. They may also think the euro is offering it a thinly veiled excuse to hike prices. Forewarned is forearmed, and whatever happens, it wants to retain the loyalty of its customers. It has therefore taken a pragmatic approach to coping with the changes that will be forthcoming.

Its first steps have been to make a checklist of all the areas it thinks will be affected by EMU, isolating areas which it thinks will be threatened and areas of new opportunities so that it can make the necessary commercial decisions before looking at the more specific practical measures that will be required to put these decisions into action. For example it's been reviewing the management of its general merchandise supply chain, store operations and management, food supply management, its European operations and its financial services business.

Initially the main input has been from its IT department and the teams that have been asked to oversee the key operating areas. M&S anticipates the software implications of the changeover will affect every aspect of its business, so it's trying to deal with Millennium issues at the same time.

So far the M&S EMU taskforce has listed a series of questions related to certain categories of its business such as customer service policy, pricing, display policy, store cash handling, supplier relationships, education and training, financial services customer accounting and financial reporting. For each question that needs to be answered it's created a matrix that will identify each area of the business that needs to be involved in the decision making and the implementation of the plan that's devised. It's also created an infallibility check to make sure that nothing is overlooked. From this it will create a list of priority actions to ensure that the most important changes are made first.

M&S has been talking to its competitors as well, all of whom are facing the same problem. It's quite extraordinary how competing businesses are working together to make sure that they're all able to deal with the euro – and the retail sector is not alone. One banker was quoted as saying that the 'level of cooperation on the street is quite incredible'.

M&S says it's also keeping its ears close to the ground to follow the progress of crucial public sector debates that will shape the enabling legislation around Europe, particularly in the field of consumer protection, with all its implications for display.

It's absolutely vital that it predicts with some accuracy how the public will react to the changes that will be forthcoming in their day-to-day lives as euros start coming into circulation and they feel them in their pockets.

IBM

IBM has announced that its conversion date to the euro will be January 2001. This will be the end of the transition period which runs from 1999 to 2001 during which companies in 'in' countries have to switch over from national currencies to the euro.

The company estimates that 80 per cent of its information technology applications will be affected by EMU. It has stated that the changeover – even using the cheap option of allowing mixed currencies until 2001 – will still be 20 per cent more expensive than addressing the Year 2000 computer problem. Peter Cruttenden, director of process management at IBM's European headquarters, has said: 'You cannot postpone the Year 2000 problem, but EMU allows you some flexibility.'

During the two year period 1999–2000 IBM's customers and suppliers will be able to settle transactions in either national currency or the euro. However, the company will continue to use the US dollar as its in-house currency even in its European operations.

BMW

The luxury car manufacturer began its preparations in 1996 and will be ready to switch operations from the deutschmark to euros from 1999. However, it is likely that it will adopt the euro step-by-step although it will put its capital on a euro basis. The switch to the euro is being combined with the adoption of a new standard software and measures to tackle the Year 2000 computer problem.

More than 60 per cent of BMW's turnover is subject to currency risk. The share of sales at risk from European currency movements will shrink with the euro to 10 per cent from 26 per cent.

Siemens

The German engineering group opened the UK's first euro-denominated bank account in March 1998 – even though the euro did not exist. It will introduce the euro as its main trading currency from January 1999 and, although it will not force its suppliers or customers to use euros, is likely to encourage firms to adopt the euro.

Bernd Euler, Siemens' UK finance director, has said: 'If 80 per cent of our customers want to be invoiced in euros, we'll want to pay 80 per cent of our bills in euros. We may then prefer a tender in euros.'

List of Euro Acronyms

EBA	European Banking Association
EC	European Commission
ECB	European Central Bank, which will be responsible for setting interest rates in euro-land and for monetary policy
ECCB	European Central Clearing Bank
ECOFIN	Council of Finance Ministers of the European Union
ECU	European Currency Unit (will be replaced by the euro on 1 January 1999)
EMI	European Monetary Institute
EMU	Economic and Monetary Union – which will create a framework for the ECB
ERM	Exchange Rate Mechanism for those countries joining the single currency in January 1999
ERM2	Exchange Rate Mechanism for countries planning to join the single currency after the first wave
ESCB	European System of Central Banks
EU	European Union
NCU	National Currency Unit
TARGET	Trans-European Automated Real-time Gross settlement Express Transfer system

Further Information

The Department of Trade and Industry has a euro preparations helpline: Tel 08456 01 01 99, and a new web site: www.euro.gov.uk
Also contact:

your bank
accountant
local chamber of commerce
local Business Link.

Internet Information

(All addresses begin with http: //)

Bank of England: euro www.bankofengland.co.uk/euro.htm
HM Treasury: www.hm-treasury.gov.uk
European Institutions: europa.eu.int/index.htm
European Commission: europa.eu.int/comm/
EMI: europa.eu.int/emi/
FEE (accounting and other information: www.euro.fee.be
IT issues: www.cordis.lu/esprit/src/wdiseuro.htm
Association for the Monetary Union of Europe: amue.if.net

Business Groups and Advisers

Business Links	0345 567 765
Federation of Small Businesses	0171 233 7900
Forum of Private Business	01565 634 467
British Chamber of Commerce	0171 565 2000
BCI	0171 389 7400
European Movement hotline	0990 011997

Attributions

Abbey Life
Arnheim & Co
Arthur Andersen
The Association for the Monetary Union of Britain
Bank of England
Barclays
Beachcroft Stanleys
British Steel
The Centre for European Reform
Clifford Chance
Confederation of British Industry (CBI)
Credit Suisse First Boston
The Department of Trade and Industry
Deutsche Bank
Economist Intelligence Unit
The European Commission
FEE
The Forum of Private Business
Goldman Sachs
Hill & Knowlton
IBM
The Institute of Directors
KPMG
Lloyds Bank
Lovell White Durrant
Merrill Lynch
JP Morgan
NatWest Bank
Paine Webber
Paribas
Price Waterhouse
The Royal Bank of Scotland
SBC Dillon Warburg
The Treasury
Vicky Mann Associates (Executive Search Consultants)
Winterthur